THE CLINICIAN'S TOOLBOX

REDISCOVERING COMPASSIONATE ABA

RONALD LEAF

JAMISON DAYHARSH

JONATHAN RAFUSE

JOHN McEACHIN

JUSTIN B. LEAF

The Clinician's Toolbox: Rediscovering Compassionate ABA
Copyright © 2023 Autism Partnership
Published by: Different Roads to Learning, Inc.
    12 West 18th Street, Suite 3E
    New York, NY 10011
    tel: 212.604.9637 | fax: 212.206.9329
    www.difflearn.com

Book Design: Sally Rinehart
Proofreader: Rosie McDonald
Cover Art: Nola V/peopleimages.com - stock.adobe.com

Library of Congress Control Number: 2023902532
ISBN: 978-0-9998753-0-8

Printed in the United States of America

FOREWORD

BY RON LEAF

I was sure that *Clinical Judgment* would be my last book. It was intended to help the new generation of behaviorists learn about some of ABA's pioneers that seemed to have been forgotten. Those that inspired us. How could I "retire" without people knowing about Joseph Wolpe, Sandra Harris and Don Baer? Recently, however, it became painfully clear that there is another area that has been sadly neglected.

Social media has been abuzz about a new movement: "compassionate behaviorism." I was perplexed! First, this group of social media bullies were discussing "compassion"! Moreover, this small group of practitioners was acting as if old concepts such as "therapeutic alliance" and being "curious listeners" were new. They seemed unaware that Carl Rodgers discussed this in 1957 and, in 1999, Richard Fox shared his deep concern that behaviorists seemed to be neglecting the crucial need for becoming "behavioral artists."

If the agenda was to rekindle this neglected area, I would have been thrilled. But it seems there is far more to their movement and that their agenda is creating tremendous collateral damage. For example, they argue that true "compassionate behaviorists" should not give corrective, or sometimes even positive, feedback. In their view, all feedback is coercion. Of course, when providing corrective feedback, one should be sensitive and thoughtful. But to avoid corrective feedback completely is absurd, and ironically, not compassionate. I wouldn't be an effective baseball coach if I didn't tell a baseball player that he needs to track the pitch and stop pulling his head. I wouldn't be an effective teacher if I didn't provide corrective feedback regarding class presentations. And I wouldn't be a good partner if I resisted listening to my wife's feedback.

These practitioners also suggest that behaviorists should completely acquiesce to the agenda of their clients[1]. That is, only work on those issues that the clients feel are important to work on. Obviously, we need to carefully listen to our clients, but often it is necessary to help our clients understand that only focusing on their top priority is not in their best interests. For example, a client may want to fix a toxic relationship, even when it's not possible and clearly not in their best interest. Or, a client may want you to help them convince their partner that it's okay for them to continue with their heavy drinking! Or that

---

[1] Throughout the text, "client" will refer to the recipient of ABA intervention, and "trainee" will refer to interventionists new to the field.

it's preferable for them not to have friends, even though the research shows this can lead to isolation, depression, suicidal ideation and suicide.

Perhaps the most disturbing aspect of this movement is that these "compassionate behaviorists" are providing guidance on how to treat trauma. In order to treat trauma, one must have extensive education, training and testing to ensure that one has the necessary skill set. Otherwise, treating someone with depression or post-traumatic stress disorder can lead to catastrophic consequences. Essentially, they are encouraging folks to practice psychology without a license which is not only a misdemeanor in many States, but it is extremely dangerous!

For me and my colleagues, it was imperative to write *The Clinician's Toolbox: Rediscovering Compassionate Behaviorism*, not only to set the record straight about behaviorist history, but to learn from the clinical pioneers, and most importantly, to share the skills necessary to become effective behaviorists. Our goal is to inspire the new generation of behaviorists to receive the necessary education and training so they can truly become talented clinicians. Our ultimate hope is for the leaders in the field of Applied Behavior Analysis to understand that clinical training must become part of educational curricula, credentialling task lists and testing. Otherwise, we are not being "compassionate behaviorists"!

CONTENTS

CHAPTER 1

COMPASSIONATE BEHAVIORISM ISN'T NEW

For years we have been outspoken regarding our concerns with the field of Applied Behavior Analysis (ABA) (J. B. Leaf et al., 2017; J. B. Leaf et al., 2022; R. Leaf et al., 2008; R. Leaf et al., 2019). These concerns are borne out of our dedication to ABA as a science, and our deep belief in the tools it provides us as practitioners for developing technologies and therapies to benefit every member of our shared society. We have committed our time, our resources and our skill to the further evolution of the field, and to the promise it has for those participating in its therapeutic course. But over the past several decades, the field we love appears to have regressed and narrowed, devolved rather than evolved, and has sacrificed much of its healing potential, its heart and soul (see *It Has to Be Said*, R. Leaf et al., 2008 and *Clinical Judgment*, R. Leaf et al., 2019).

As we discussed in *Clinical Judgment*, our founding mothers and fathers were curious, innovative, calculated risk-takers and talented clinicians. They were trained not only in general psychology, but also in applied clinical skills. Joseph Wolpe, Sandra Harris, and Mont Wolf fully understood the concepts of therapeutic alliance and "active listening" as applied to their groundbreaking work and study. While they explored and deepened the ABA knowledge base, they were systematic, careful and humane. They had utmost concern for the welfare of their clients and instilled those values in their protegees, hoping to ensure the legacy would endure beyond their lifetime. They valued and utilized sensitivity, empathy and compassion as critical components of promoting socially valid skills in their clients.

In the book *A History of The Behavioral Therapies* (2001), the authors shared:

> *"Knowing where we came from allows us to assess whether we have lost something; whether we have drifted away from some of the strengths that allowed us to be where we are today." (O'Donohue et al., 2002, p. xv)*

> *"A valuable lesson may be that some of what made behavior therapy successful has been lost across generations." (O'Donohue et al., 2002, p. xv)*

Professional practice within the field of ABA has become narrowly applied over the years. Although the establishment of the Behavior Analyst Certification Board (BACB) has provided some minimum training and experience standards and codification of ethics, its creation has also diminished the spirit of innovation. For example, as we all know, the demand for qualified practitioners has exploded since the late 1990s, resulting from heightened public recognition and interest in serving children with autism spectrum disorder (ASD). The need to rapidly increase the supply of interventionists has resulted in simplifying, diluting, manualizing and providing training that is too limited in scope. The skill level of those newly minted practitioners does not match the complexity of needs among the population being served. Thus, the intervention provided by this level of professional has become more regimented and protocol-driven, less clinically sophisticated, and sometimes harmful over both the short- and long-term.

Tragically, for someone wanting to practice ABA as an interventionist, training duration has become time- rather than performance-based. Typically, staff receive between 40 and 80 hours of training and take a multiple-choice exam on limited content area in order to qualify as a Registered Behavior Technician® (RBT®) (see J. B. Leaf et al., 2021). While a supervising Board-Certified Behavior Analyst (BCBA) must sign off that they are competent in specific skills, the skill inventory is limited, and there is little assurance about what constitutes an adequate level of performance and competency. This is hypocrisy. Providing effective, professional, therapeutically beneficial treatment is a highly sophisticated skill set. Would you be comfortable flying with a pilot who has limited training exposure to challenging weather conditions or incorrect instrument readings, or was not extensively trained on the plane they are flying today? Would you trust a chef who has only taken a series of classes online, passed a virtual test and then prepared you a main course of blowfish (which is deadly if not prepared correctly)?

Because the training and experience has become so narrow and limited, intervention has become largely protocol-driven and thus formulaic and rigid. ABA therapy has been reduced to a robotic assembly line with canned target behaviors and skills; scripted instructions; prompting methods that are prescribed at the beginning of the month and may not be updated for weeks; reinforcer selection that is determined at 8:30 a.m. and does not change for the rest of the day; strict protocols defining when to move phases; and time-consuming data collection that does not result in immediate adjustment to the teaching methods. There is a lack of forethought, individualization, collaboration with the client or family, and most concerning, no connectivity between curricular components or how those components lead to a plan for teaching generalization and greater independence. It's a travesty of lost opportunity, and in some cases results in outright harm. We are greatly disturbed that intervention often is not comprehensive and therefore doesn't address critical issues such as self-advocacy, leisure and recreation skills, independent living and, most importantly, social skills. It's no wonder ABA has lost its luster over the past several decades. This is evidenced by a growing frustration and pushback from a wide segment of the population (see J. B. Leaf et al., 2021 and Gorycki et al., 2020 for overview of the frustration). And to be frank, some of those voices expressing opposition to ABA treatment are right to complain and should be listened to. Our field requires a clinical, expert course correction.

This is not the way it started out. The field seems to have forgotten the power and art of effective teaching strategies such as shaping (Cihon, 2022). Instead, the preponderance of training and thus intervention promotes prompting and devalues shaping as a tool to promote growth in skills and increasing independence in our clients. Shaping is a difficult skill to master, but when used correctly, this technique is highly efficient. Similarly, respondent conditioning (Watson & Rayner, 1920) has been greatly minimized. Therefore, because this critical knowledge is not included in most training protocols, interventionists often see emotional behavior as simply operant and then don't provide the proper intervention to promote dealing with frustration, stress and anxiety in an appropriate manner. The skill set promoting greater clinical assessment in our therapists, both in-the-moment and in general, has been forgotten. Thus, treatment is less tailored to the individual and less responsive to their continually varying behavior, potentially dooming the client to a less optimal and less fulfilling outcome.

We have engaged in both private communication and public discourse (J. B. Leaf et al., 2017; J.B. Leaf., 2022; R. Leaf et al., 2008) with the BACB about our concerns. We have urged a greatly expanded scope and focus of the BCBA task list (Behavior Analyst Certification Board, 2017). This alone would impact what curriculum is included and being taught in a master's program in ABA, and ultimately would impact the BCBA credentialling exam by making it more comprehensive and realistic, more like what fledgling interventionists would have to be prepared for in the real world. We have discussed at length the importance of interventionists being trained and tested in clinical skills. This requires more time, more effort, and more expense. It is not an easy path to navigate, and there are likely many variables to consider. But historically, these clinical skills have been key components to providing the level of therapeutic service we all should expect, the service our families deserve. Anything less is a disservice. The mission of behavior analysts is to assist people in need, to achieve socially meaningful behavior change, and that requires empathy, sensitivity and compassion. Without this skill set it is very difficult to completely understand and connect with the clients we serve, the parents we work with, and the professional community we interact with.

I (Ron Leaf) was attending a prestigious conference of top professionals in the field of ASD. There was a workshop regarding working with parents. The topic came up about parents not following recommendations and what should be done about it. Tragically, there was no discussion or understanding of why parents may not follow recommendations. No understanding that perhaps parents are overwhelmed, or what is being recommended is not a top priority, or that they are deeply saddened about their child and want them only to be happy. From a behavioral standpoint, they were not assessing the functions of the behavior that they labeled as "non-compliance".

I was shocked. Their complete lack of understanding of the challenges that parents face, their absolute lack of sensitivity, was appalling. Moreover, the apparent lack of training they had received regarding the clinical issues that parents face was glaring. After taking several deep breaths and fruitlessly trying to use guided imagery, I blurted out that perhaps we should follow the literature on "non-compliance" and punish parents. The group quickly agreed with my preposterous suggestion, not recognizing my sarcasm. Not surprising, because they didn't show evidence of having an ounce of clinical skills. They actually asked what kind of punishment I would suggest. I quickly said perhaps time-out or firm reprimands. They then asked how they should implement those suggestions!

To quote Barack Obama, "We have to do better." We must train interventionists to be clinicians. Clinical skills must be part of the training and testing. We owe it to interventionists, children, families and the field.

WHY WE WROTE THIS BOOK

We are passionate about working with children with ASD and their families. We love training folks new and old who have the potential to greatly impact these children, adolescents and adults. We embrace working with parents and feel they are truly the most critical contributors to the treatment process. And we cherish the field. After all, it has been our life's work.

But we are clearly frustrated with many professionals' low expectations and lack of appreciation for what can be accomplished with truly quality treatment. Too many parents have been told to accept that their child will not be able to be conversational, have friends, or graduate from high school. We are distraught that the new generation of interventionists is not receiving the training, supervision and support that they so dearly deserve and require. We are dismayed that parents are not receiving the support that they desperately desire and need. We are appalled that the field we love has so ignored our rich history. Concepts of "therapeutic alliance," "active listening" and "compassion" are now considered innovative. But our vast historic record is peppered with research, books, and scholarly articles both defining these critical concepts and showing over and over how critical they are to providing the most effective treatment available. Thus, we are deeply saddened that education, training and testing in clinical skills has been largely abandoned.

We are hoping that this book will not only correct the record, but be a helpful resource for new interventionists, more seasoned veterans and parents. We are writing for these three audiences because "it takes a village." We understand that those passionate individuals wanting a comprehensive training package to better serve their clients and families are not to blame. The underlying issues lie squarely at the feet of the system, a system that is clearly overwhelmed. The demand is high, and the supply is low. But that is not excuse enough to allow the current state of affairs to continue; again, we must do better!

Our intent is to provide informed guidance for our three audiences. We don't want to just vent, but to be part of the solution. We yearn for the day when interventionists are not only masterful in teaching essential skills using their clinical judgment to make rapid changes, but they are also sensitive and compassionate clinicians.

References

Behavior Analyst Certification Board. (2017). BCBA task list (5th ed.). Littleton, CO: Author.

Cihon, J. H. (2022). Shaping: A brief history, research overview, and recommendations. In J.B. Leaf, J. H. Cihon, J. L. Ferguson, & M. J. Weiss (2022). *Handbook of Applied Behavior Analysis Intervention for Autism*. Cham, Switzerland: Springer.

Gorycki, K.A., Ruppel, P.R., Zane, T. (2020) Is long-term ABA therapy abusive: A response to Sandoval-Norton and Shkedy, Cogent Psychology, 7:1.

Leaf, J.B., Cihon, J.H., Leaf, R., McEachin, J., Liu, N., Russell, N., Unumb, L., Shapiro, S., Khosrowshahi, D., 2021(b). Concerns about ABA-based intervention: An evaluation and recommendations. *Journal of Autism and Developmental Disorders*. doi:10.1007/s10803-021-05137-y

Leaf, J. B., Leaf, R., McEachin, J., Bondy, A., Cihon, J. H., Detrich, R., Eshleman, J., Ferguson, J. L., Foxx, R. M., Freeman, B. J., Gerhardt, P., Glenn, S. S., Miller, M., Milne, C. M., Mountjoy, T., Parker, T., Prtichard, J., Ross, R. K., Saunders, M. S., & Streff, T. (2021). The importance of professional discourse for the continual advancement of practice standards, The RBT® as a case in point. *Journal of Autism and Developmental Disorders*, 51, 1780-1801.

Leaf, J. B., Leaf, R., McEachin, J., Taubman, M., Smith, T., Harris, S. L., Freeman, B. J., Mountjoy, T., Parker, T., Streff, T., Volkmar, F. R., & Waks, A. (2017). Concerns about the registered behavior technician™ in relation to effective autism intervention. *Behavior Analysis in Practice*, 10(2), 154–163. https://doi.org/10.1007/s40617-016-0145-9

Leaf, R. B.,McEachin, J. J., & Taubman, M. (2008). *Sense and nonsense in the behavioral treatment of autism: It has to be said.* New York,NY: DRL Books.

Leaf, R., Taubman, M., Bondy, A., & McEachin, J. (2008b). To BCBA or not to B? In R. Leaf, J.McEachin, & M. Taubman (Eds.), *Sense and nonsense in the behavioral treatment of autism: It has to be said* (pp. 47–54). New York: Different Roads to Learning.

Leaf, R., Leaf, J. B., & McEachin, J. (2019). *Clinical judgment in ABA: Lessons from our pioneers.* New York: Different Roads to Learning.

O'Donohue, W. T., Henderson, D., Hayes, S. C., Fisher, J., & Hayes, J. (2001). *A history of the behavioral therapies: Founder's personal histories* (1st Edition). Oakland, CA: Context Press.

Watson, J. B., & Rayner, R. (1920). Conditioned emotional reactions. *Journal of Experimental Psychology*, 3(1), 1.

CHAPTER 2

BECOMING A CLINICIAN

RON LEAF

My Mom was an extremely nurturing preschool teacher and my Dad graduated with a degree in Psychology from UCLA. My parents were extremely liberal and oozed the importance of compassion for all of humanity. They were outspoken about the mistreatment of the disenfranchised. As a seven-year-old, I worked on political campaigns for a candidate who reflected their values. Stamping envelopes and displaying political badges were my duties. These experiences were incredibly important in shaping my values. In retrospect it's not surprising that I became a psychologist. I was the one that befriended classmates new to my school. And I was the designated listener to friends when they were upset. I sought out those who were lonely and needed support.

Although I was a political science major at UCLA with the hope of becoming a politician in the spirit of FDR, Adlai Stevenson and Eugene McCarthy, my life direction quickly changed when I took Ivar Lovaas's undergraduate Behavior Modification class in 1973. Ivar was captivating and the work he was doing was mind-blowing. It was an exciting time in autism and ABA. There was amazing progress in overcoming the challenges of juvenile delinquency, "hyperactivity," anorexia, depression, etc. I decided I wanted to be a part of this amazing field!

I went to Southern Illinois University to earn my master's degree and learned about kindness and compassion from Tony Cuvo and Roger Poppin. I took classes from some of the top behaviorists whose expertise was quite varied. Harry Rubin was a leading researcher in sexuality. Nate Azrin focused on areas including intellectual impairment, tics, self-injury and job hunting. Richard Sanders' interest was primarily in alcoholism. I learned that ABA was applicable across ages and populations. But most notably, I learned that quality ABA had to be practiced with clinical sensitivity.

I was fortunate enough to return to UCLA to earn my Ph.D. in psychology and was extremely fortunate to once again work with Ivar. Most people think of Ivar as being a staunch behaviorist who relied on punishment. What they may not know is that intervention at UCLA was based primarily upon reinforcement. Moreover, we were not protocol-driven in the slightest. As Ivar continuously implored:

"If the learner does not learn in the way we teach, then we must teach in the way they learn."

What people also may not know is that Ivar was originally trained in psychoanalysis. He was the consummate clinician. I marveled at how clinically adept he was. He was vehement in his opinion that his graduate students needed to become clinicians. He insisted that we were trained in general psychology that included extensive training in clinical skills. We needed to fully understand how to interpret the Rorschach and MMPI and know the works of Freud, Rogers and Piaget. We had to be skilled in active listening, therapeutic alliance and compassion.

I learned about the importance of clinical skills from Ivar. I took classes from Andy Christensen, whose expertise was using the foundations of ABA to work with marital discord and family dynamics. Bruce Baker's expertise was training and empowering parents of children with developmental disabilities. Barbara Henker was a Developmental Psychologist who taught us about child development and the stress families experience from having children with developmental disabilities. She promoted using a behavioral framework to formulate coping skills. Frank Hewett's expertise was how to work in school systems with a compassionate perspective. These were all amazing mentors!

Early in my career I provided parent education and support to mothers, fathers and care providers who had children, adolescents and adults with developmental disabilities. My job was to provide meaningful information and help them develop their skills so that they would be more effective in dealing with behavioral challenges and helping their child/client acquire skills in multiple areas.

Perhaps the single most life changing clinical event occurred when I was working with a mom who had a three-year-old "precocious" child. The presenting problem was that her child threw his waffles on the floor from his highchair each morning. It totally disrupted the flow of the morning and she felt helpless and hopeless. I quickly gave her some "brilliant" suggestions, including using reinforcement and providing minimal attention to his throwing the waffles. She seemed quite impressed with my "brilliance."

During our next session she reported that the suggestions worked beautifully with the waffles, but what should she do when he threw his toast on the floor? I was flabbergasted. I couldn't fathom how she didn't see it as an identical situation and to simply apply my same brilliant suggestions. But upon reflection, I realized that it was totally my fault. By prescribing what to do I had created dependency and had not made her part of the process. Furthermore, I had not provided her with the foundation or rationale for my suggestions. Her inability to "generalize" the information was due to my incompetence. She was the learner who did not learn in the way I was teaching, so it was on me to figure out how to "teach in the way the learner can learn!"

I recognized that I simply did not have the clinical skill set to help the parents I was serving. I immediately sought out help. I connected with a psychotherapist, Marilyn, who had an extensive background in behaviorism but eventually became psychodynamic in her orientation. She had a large private practice in which she saw a large variety of clientele. Marilyn was simply an amazing therapist and mentor. I, my fellow author Jamie Dayharsh, and a group of behavior therapists went through extensive training on clinical skills. Eventually we conducted therapy with individuals with depression and couples in marital distress. Marilyn taught me clinical life lessons that became part of my fabric.

LESSONS LEARNED

One of the first lessons I learned was the importance of nonverbal communication. For example, Marilyn taught me to pay careful attention to when couples walked in the door. Who was first walking in? Were they holding hands, did they sit close together, how did they look at each other, what were their facial responses when the other talked? What did their facial expressions and body language show? She emphasized this was every bit as important as what they were saying. It provided information about their relationship, their areas of agreement and disagreement, their happiness and sadness. It helped you understand if they agreed or disagreed with each other. Often nonverbal communication was more accurate and important than verbal communication.

She taught me the importance of asking questions, because everyone experiences life differently. I was encouraged to never assume or imagine I knew what they meant when they spoke. If they said they were "depressed," I would ask them how their sadness manifested itself. Some people sleep constantly when they are depressed, some sleep very little. Eating is extremely different among those who are depressed. I learned not to assume based on my own experiences. I had to ask questions, seek clarification. I had to fully understand their perspective, be a curious, sensitive and compassionate listener.

A very difficult lesson was about determining and exposing the source of a client's pain; getting to the root of the problem. Once again, I had to pay careful attention to body language. I learned that when you see a client's eyes tearing up, you have most likely found a source of pain, potentially a foundational issue to explore. And being compassionate meant fully discussing their pain. Marilyn called it "going for the kill." Obviously, helpful intervention depends on timing and has to be done with complete sensitivity. You need to validate their pain. You must understand their perspective and share in it. And you can't rush through the process.

It seemed so counterintuitive that exposing and then exploring the pain was actually being compassionate. But I learned that is how we can make meaningful change. Marilyn emphasized that it was not our job to make clients happy in the short run. If we don't nudge them to expose and deal with their ghosts, we are colluding with them in avoidance. She cautioned us not to be like the novice or naive therapists who avoid this at all costs. She would say, be a "mature therapist."

The importance of being an outstanding listener seemed obvious. Not only was it intuitive but it was a topic often discussed in my classes at UCLA. Nonetheless, I never realized just how complex a skill set this is, and I learned that there are therapeutic blockers that result in therapists being poor listeners. For example, taking notes and having a set agenda can give the impression that you are not really listening.

Marilyn stressed that when your client is sharing their pain, don't problem-solve. Being in the helping field, it is a natural tendency. But typically, when people are talking about their grief and experiencing pain, they don't want answers; they just want you to listen and feel their anguish. Active listening is a critical concept requiring a deeper dive in a later chapter.

Therapeutic alliance was an ongoing training focus. Marilyn discussed the research (e.g., Rogers, 1957) informing her clinical experience; she considered it such an important aspect of therapy. The therapist being relatable was an essential factor in successful therapy and contributed to better outcomes for clients. Therefore, chatting with your clients, being personable and sincerely interested in their life was crucial. Some of her guidelines included speaking the language that they use and avoiding jargon. If they were "artsy" in their communication, then you needed to be "artsy." If they were from the world of science, then talk in that manner. Therapeutic alliance will be covered in a subsequent chapter.

Marilyn emphasized one of our primary missions was to help the client see themselves accurately. She used the analogy that as a therapist you hold a mirror for your clients (your words, your perspective), and that you use this mirror to help them see their strengths, their flaws and their issues. Your questions, comments and reflections were your mirror. You had to figure out how and when to adjust the mirror, to bring their process into greater focus. Sometimes you could quickly bring the mirror to their face, but more often it was a gradual process. You had to be highly nuanced in having them see themselves in the mirror so that they could accept the vision. In essence it was having them see and accept the reality of their situation. Only then could they gain enough insight to begin developing remedies.

Perhaps the most valuable lesson was about leading clients to the answer. Marilyn emphasized that telling them the answer was often counterproductive. She talked about the principle of cognitive dissonance. I naively thought I understood cognitive dissonance through my studies (e.g., Festinger, 1957). But she related it to therapy. In essence, if clients came up with the answer, they were far more likely to be interested in making change. The therapist's job was to skillfully lead them to the answer. And if you were really good at it, it meant the client had no idea that you were part of the process. You could tell you did a great job when your client got annoyed paying your bill, since they did all the work! Marilyn said, "You have to leave your ego at the door." If you didn't do this, your therapy would suffer, and in the end, you weren't going to look brilliant, nor were you going to get accolades.

She stressed that you must strive to be an active listener. She discussed the work of Carl Rogers, that in essence he was shaping clients through his reflective approach. This was certainly borne out by Truax's research (e.g., 1966). From her guidance we then developed the psychoeducational approach. We learned that being prescriptive—telling clients what to do—had its place in certain situations, but that there are distinct disadvantages. Most notably, it diminishes client buy-in and therefore follow-through.

REDISCOVERY

The concepts of active listening, therapeutic alliance and compassion within the field of ABA are *not* new concepts. Mary Cover Jones, Joseph Wolpe, Sandra Harris and Mont Wolf embodied these concepts and applied them to their groundbreaking work and study. While they explored and deepened the ABA knowledge base, they were systematic, careful and humane. Their foremost concern was the welfare of those they were serving and they intended this to be foundational to the field. They valued and utilized sensitivity, empathy and compassion as critical components to the promotion of socially valid skills in their clients. Hans Miller's parent training model demonstrated the importance of interventionists having clinical skill (1975). Richard Foxx wrote of the importance of "behavioral artistry," and fully discussed the clinical skill set that was vital in providing quality intervention (1996).

Tragically, the field today seems to have ignored our past. It has taken us away from our roots. Moreover, it has compromised the lives of clients and their families. The literature is full of the skills that are necessary to become a virtuoso clinician. We are thrilled that currently there is a rediscovery of clinical skills and a movement to help behaviorists understand the need to be compassionate (LeBlanc et al., 2020; Taylor et al., 2018). What is sad is that it's being portrayed as if it's a new discovery (Miller, 2021). Active listening, therapeutic alliance and compassion are not new ideas in the slightest! We don't have to reinvent the wheel, but we can certainly make it better, and maybe this time we can make it stick.

This book is devoted to discussing clinical skills in the hopes of helping interventionists, families, professionals and the field of ABA.

References

Festinger, L. (1957). *A theory of cognitive dissonance*. Stanford University Press.

Foxx R.M. Translating the covenant: The behavior analyst as ambassador and translator. *The Behavior Analyst*. 1996;19:147–161.

LeBlanc, L.A., Taylor, B.A. & Marchese, N.V. (2020). The Training Experiences of Behavior Analysts: Compassionate Care and Therapeutic Relationships with Caregivers. *Behavior Analysis Practice* 13, 387–393 https://doi.org/10.1007/s40617-019-00368-z

Miller, M. (2021, June). *Compassionately assessing challenging behavior*. Invited presentation for Luna ABA. Online.

Miller, W. H.: *Systematic parent training: Procedures, cases and issues*. Champaign, Ill.: Research Press, 1975.

Rogers C.R. (1957). The necessary and sufficient conditions of therapeutic personality change. *Journal of Consulting Psychology*, 21, 95-103.

Taylor, B. A., LeBlanc, L. A., & Nosik, M. R. (2018). Compassionate care in behavior analytic treatment: Can outcomes be enhanced by attending to relationships with caregivers? *Behavior Analysis in Practice*. Advance online publication. doi: 10.1007/s40617-018-00289-3

Truax, C.B. (1966). Reinforcement and nonreinforcement in Rogerian psychotherapy. *Journal of Abnormal Psychology*, 71, 1-9.

CHAPTER 3

THERAPEUTIC ALLIANCE

When building a therapeutic alliance, the clinical components of empathy, compassion and unconditional positive regard are critical. A common pillar of therapeutic alliance includes reaching agreement on treatment goals and establishing and sharing the direction of therapy. An overarching principle is to help your client feel welcome and safe within the process and not make them feel judged. Building the therapeutic alliance means being masterful at perspective-taking. It means that you resonate with the wide range of emotions that your client is expressing, and you truly mirror their emotions as they are expressed in therapy. It's okay to share your sadness with what they have experienced, or to fully share in their triumphs, to laugh with them. It's all about validating and normalizing what they have experienced.

So, what are the steps of building a durable therapeutic alliance with the client? What clinical skills have been shown to lead to a greater connection with the client, and a better outcome? Let's take a more detailed look at the history and the implications for our current clinical work. In the 1970s, I (Ron) took a class at Southern Illinois from a world-renowned behaviorist. He was brilliant, applied ABA across varied populations, and treated critical problems facing children, adolescents and adults. Unfortunately, he had tremendous disdain for other schools of psychology. He referred to them as being squishy or too "touchy feely." He talked about the silliness of chit-chatting with your clients at the beginning of sessions. It was his belief that the second a client entered your office you immediately start the tough work and that you should never waste precious time being superfluous!

Who was I to argue? I was a novice, and this was a top behavioral superstar. But the approach he was professing seemed cold and uncaring. From a radical behavioral perspective, I questioned how such a therapist would become a social reinforcer, which seemed to be so very important. It seemed reminiscent of John B. Watson's off-putting recommendation to parents regarding affection (Watson, 1928):

> *"If you must, kiss them once on the forehead when they say goodnight. Shake hands with them in the morning." (Watson, 1928, p. 81).*

Fortunately, I soon started taking classes, reading books and articles regarding clinical skills, and then conducted therapy while receiving extensive training and feedback. I fondly remember reading a book in which the authors attempted to identify the best predictor of positive therapeutic outcomes. They examined variables such as age of the therapist, gender, education, training, years of experience and psychological orientation. Of all the considerations they examined, the factor that was most predictive was the connection with the therapist, i.e., the "therapeutic alliance." In short, it is the culmination of planning, clinical sensitivity, empathy and attentive listening.

There are hundreds of research articles dating back to the 1950s concluding that the most important factor in successful therapeutic outcomes was indeed the therapeutic relationship. Depending upon psychological orientation (e.g., Behavioral, Freudian, or Rogerian), different terms were used to describe what we refer to as therapeutic alliance, but it all boils down to the therapist being able to relate to the client. John Dollard and Neal Miller (1950), leading behaviorists of the time, emphasized the importance of the social conditions of learning. Bruce Wampold and colleagues have conducted extensive research on the factors that contribute to the efficacy of psychotherapy (2000, 2008, 2010). He found that the differences among various treatments were essentially very small or even nonexistent. He found that the most important factor was the interpersonal relationship with the therapist. Once again, therapeutic alliance is essential.

In his 1998 article on behavioral artistry (BA), Richard Foxx described many elements of artistry including liking people, perceptual sensitivity, and humor. These are parallel to the elements of therapeutic alliance: compassion, and active listening. Unfortunately, his brilliant ideas were overlooked, so much so that more than 20 years later he published a follow-up article, again beseeching the importance of behavioral artistry (Callahan et al., 2019). The authors found that parents of children with ASD preferred therapists with BA. They also showed that interventionists that had higher scores of BA were more effective therapists. Unfortunately, however, those working in the field of ABA had lower levels of behavioral artistry than those in other human service professions. They also commented:

"The repertoires of today's behavior analysts can lack essential interpersonal behaviors related to the optimal delivery and outcome of ABA services." (Callahan et al., 2019, p. 10.)

Preparing for therapy at the outset is critical. We want to set the occasion for the development of trust, no matter what the client brings to the table. So, building a therapeutic alliance starts with a sound and collaborative plan. Having a general plan and a guiding philosophy will define the expectations of the therapy. The therapist can shape buy-in by partnering with the client in the development of the therapy plan. Within that plan there is always room for flexibility and the plan should be modified as you progress toward the goal or encounter unanticipated glitches.

In addition to having a general plan, the therapist must strive to be approachable and relatable, right from the get-go. Anticipate the client and the "culture" they bring to the room. In addition to mental, emotional and structural readiness, sometimes being prepared is about the way you present yourself. Should you dress casually, or should you be a little more formally dressed? I can always tell by the jewelry my wife is wearing the lifestyle of the client she was going to see. There are subtle adjustments we can make to de-emphasize youthfulness when age difference may be a potential barrier, just as a more senior clinician can make adjustments to become more approachable to younger clientele. We once had a therapist who had the natural appearance of a runway model. She understood her clients (and other staff) may be intimidated or make assumptions that could impact how well they relate to her and was careful to play down the stereotype. Of course, you may not have the full picture of your client before you first meet them, but take your best guess based upon the information you have already gathered and then adjust once you have had your first session.

Examples of preparedness contributing to the development of therapeutic alliance abound. When I was at UCLA, Dennis Russo did a presentation on his work in child pediatrics. Dennis worked closely with Ivar during his graduate days. He was a published researcher, brilliant, and charismatic. After receiving his Ph.D., he eventually changed his field of concentration from autism to working with children with cancer and helping them with pain management. He was intriguing and inspiring while discussing the application of ABA to this population. But what struck me about his lecture was when he talked about how critical it was to be able to relate to the children he was serving! He shared that the most important "work time" for him was Saturday mornings. That's when he watched cartoons so that he could completely understand children's interests and passions so that he could begin every interaction discussing the latest episodes. He fully recognized how critical it was to be relatable and therefore build therapeutic alliance.

In our early days of Autism Partnership, one of our exceptional therapists, Nadine, exemplified the "Russo method." She would spend her weekends going to local parks with a thermos of coffee and the newspaper. While she was drinking her coffee and reading the paper, she was observing children playing so that she could better understand children's interests, how they played and interacted.

Ultimately, embarking on the journey together and beginning the critical process of entering a therapeutic alliance requires preparation, study, and a willingness to be as present as possible. Winging it is not an option and will likely result in an awkward introduction, perhaps negatively impacting the course of treatment even before the work begins.

Once the therapist has prepared thoughtfully, other considerations arise. Perhaps the most important moments within a session, whether it's parent education or psychotherapy, are the beginning and the end. At the beginning of the session, it is critical for the clients to feel comfortable, welcome and safe, thus eager to do the important work. But rather than rush that agenda, perhaps it starts with "catching up," an opportunity to maintain relatability and provide a segue from the end of the last session to the present. I fondly remember Mr. Hurley, my trigonometry teacher in high school. He would start every class with a recap of sports from the previous day. At the time we didn't recognize his genius, but we did enjoy the brief diversion from the hard work that would ensue. Because of his willingness to set us at ease, to engage with us first before getting to the difficult task at hand, we all loved him and eventually developed a love of trigonometry. He clearly understood the concept of starting with an enjoyable conversation, creating an engaging atmosphere and then building behavioral momentum. It greatly reduced our resistance to doing the tough work.

Similarly, the end of the session is critical. You want to end on a positive note, if possible, with a specific nod to the progress made either during the session or the course of treatment so far. This increases the likelihood that they will be eager for the next session. It's akin to making par on the 18th hole. You are excited to play another round regardless of how difficult the first 17 holes were. Ending on a positive note inspires the client to continue the tough work and accomplish the goals that they want to accomplish. It highlights their progress up to that point and leaves them looking forward to the next session.

INSTILLING CONFIDENCE

In order to form an effective alliance with a client or trainee, they need to have confidence in your expertise. They need to know that whatever the concern, whatever the problem, we can tackle it and make headway. If you don't believe in yourself, then the client never will. If they don't believe you have something to offer, then why would they listen to you? Research has demonstrated that expectancy is critical to successful outcomes. Expectancy is the anticipation of a desirable outcome, the hope for the light at the end of the tunnel. In 1957, JD Frank suggested that the beliefs and attitudes a client brings to sessions are important to the course and positive outcome of their therapy. If the therapist does not reflect back a sense of calm and unflappability, this can heighten a client's or a trainee's anxiety and reduce their willingness to take chances in the face of uncertainty. Self-confidence is directly related to the client's belief that you can indeed be a valuable source of information and change.

Projecting confidence isn't always easy. You may work with someone who is older, more experienced, or who holds more degrees. Sometimes you may be working with a client who is actually an expert in the field of ABA. Regardless, you still offer a different and potentially more objective perspective than the client, and that is extremely valuable. Even if they are experts, they can benefit from someone who is younger or even has less expertise and brings an unjaded attitude to the process. We often think of professional athletes who have coaches that do not have the same athletic skill as their players. Michael Jordan, Jim Brown and Sandy Koufax all had coaches that provided them with invaluable recommendations and guidance, even though those coaches could never accomplish what those players did on the field.

When working with trainees you will doubtless encounter some who are already better or more fluent in certain aspects of their professional work than you are. And if they are not there yet, your goal should be for them to become better than you, not to remain in your shadow. Marilyn was right (see Chapter 2), to be an effective clinician you must leave your ego at the door.

Also remember that you can draw on the expertise and support from your colleagues. You are part of a team and not everyone has to be an expert in everything. We also should continually strive to develop professionally just as we are promoting the professional development of our trainees. You must always work to hone your skills; you must accept that no matter how much we know, there is always more to learn.

THERAPEUTIC ALLIANCE BLOCKERS

As was mentioned previously, taking notes can be a therapeutic blocker. It can convey that you are not engaged with the client, not fully participatory in the process they are experiencing. While that is certainly not the intent of the therapist, it can appear that way. Taking notes potentially interferes with body language hindering the conveyance of attentive listening and empathy. It can also be perceived as being evaluative. The client may start to pay attention to when you are writing and wonder what it is they said that was noteworthy. "What did I say?" "What is my therapist thinking?" "Am I that badly damaged?"

This type of rumination can influence whether the client continues to be completely forthcoming and trusting of the process. It can simply break the flow.

We understand that often notes are for the purpose of being able to remember details from the session. You simply need to figure out a way to increase your memory. Perhaps the moment your client leaves you quickly put your recollections of the session to paper. Perhaps a mnemonic would be helpful, anchoring your recollections with specific words or gestures from your client, or to specific times within the session, then writing those memories down after the client has departed. Marilyn, our clinical mentor, acknowledged that young therapists fear they will forget. But if you are truly listening you will remember. She was so right!

Another potential blocker to establishing a therapeutic alliance has to do with receiving gifts. The BACB's ethical code was recently revised so that a BCBA can receive a gift of $10.00 of value or under, with good reason (Behavior Analyst Certification Board, 2020). Expressions of gratefulness can be important to acknowledge. And gifts may be culturally important, even mandatory for maintaining a trusting, professional relationship with a client. But if they are giving you a gift during the holidays as a token of their appreciation, we feel it is simply rude not to graciously accept such a gift of small monetary value. Not accepting a nominal gift makes you look rude and unappreciative, and it can damage the therapeutic relationship. Similarly, if the gift is extravagant then it would likely change the relationship (e.g., now you owe them). Therefore, expensive gifts should not be accepted.

A third blocker is working with a client/trainee whom you simply don't like. Marilyn would share that, sooner or later, you will encounter a client that you cannot find anything likeable about. There are lots of possible reasons. Perhaps they remind you too much of an obnoxious relative. Perhaps they have engaged in some despicable behaviors, such as being abusive to their children or their partner. Marilyn's advice was if you have strong negative feelings toward a client, you cannot be a source of comfort and help. So, what do you do?

Marilyn's suggestion was to try to gain a sympathetic understanding of how they got to where they are. What variables occurred that elicited the response, no matter how awful? What challenges did they face? How were they victimized? Completely put yourself in their place so that you can better understand and thus relate to them. However, if you still cannot then you should help them find another therapist.

THE TAKEAWAY

Therapeutic alliance is not a new concept whatsoever, it's just that it has come back into vogue. Unfortunately, it is not a subject discussed in ABA graduate programs. It is not a standard part of training, and experience is not a requirement for becoming a certified behavior analyst, nor is there any assessment for this skill. So, it's not surprising that so many ABA interventionists and supervisors lack this skill set. Let's do better!

References

Behavior Analyst Certification Board. (2020). *Ethics code for behavior analysts.* Littleton, CO: Author.

Callahan, K., Foxx, R.M., Swierczynski, A., Aerts, X., Mehta, S., McComb, M.E., Nichols, S.M., Segal, G., Donald, A., Sharma, R. Behavioral Artistry: Examining the Relationship Between the Interpersonal Skills and Effective Practice Repertoires of Applied Behavior Analysis Practitioners. J Autism Dev Disord. 2019 Sep;49(9):3557-3570. doi: 10.1007/s10803-019-04082-1. Erratum in: J Autism Dev Disord. 2019 Aug 28;: PMID: 31127484; PMCID: PMC6707962.

Dollard, J., & Miller, N. E. (1950). Personality and Psychotherapy: An Analysis in Terms of Learning, Thinking, and Culture. New York: McGraw-Hill.

Imel, Z. E., & Wampold, B. E. (2008). The importance of treatment and the science of common factors in psychotherapy. *Handbook of counseling psychology, 4,* 249-266.

Foxx, R. M. (1998). Twenty-five years of applied behavior analysis: Lessons learned. Discriminant, 4, 13–31.

Frank, J. D. (1957). Some determinants, manifestations, and effects of cohesiveness in therapy groups. *International Journal of Group Psychotherapy, 7,* 53–63.

Wampold, B. E. (2000). Outcomes of individual counseling and psychotherapy: Empirical evidence addressing two fundamental questions. In S. D. Brown & R. W. Lent (Eds.), *Handbook of counseling psychology,* (pp. 711–739).

Watson, J. B. (1928). *Psychological care of infant and child.* W. W. Norton & Co.

Zuroff, D. C., Kelly, A. C., Leybman, M. J., Blatt, S. J., & Wampold, B. E. (2010). Between-therapist and within-therapist differences in the quality of the therapeutic relationship: Effects on maladjustment and self-critical perfectionism. *Journal of Clinical Psychology, 66*(7), 681-697.

CHAPTER 4

ACTIVE LISTENING

"Active listening refers to a pattern of listening that keeps you engaged with your conversation partner in a positive way. It is the process of listening attentively while someone else speaks, paraphrasing and reflecting back what is said, and withholding judgment and advice." (Poll everywhere, n.d.)

Carl Rogers and Richard Farson coined the term "active listening" in 1957. Like therapeutic alliance and compassion, it is not a new concept, but has recently been rediscovered by a younger generation of behavior analysts as an essential missing ingredient (Kolu, 2022; LeBlanc et al., 2020; Miller, 2021; Rajaraman et al., 2022; Sadavoy et al., 2021; Taylor et al., 2018). The pioneer behavior analysts were well-rounded clinicians and understood that active listening was an essential part of the assessment process. They understood that being attentive and reflective go a long way toward establishing rapport and trust. We all can relate to how important feeling understood is in our personal relationships. Being too quick to attempt problem-solving derails the process of communication and it becomes a primary area of conflict and distress. *"I just want my partner to listen. I'm not seeking their advice and I don't need them to problem-solve. Just listen and please at least act like you are interested and care!"* As mental health professionals we need to do the same: Listen! Being an active listener helps build therapeutic alliance.

ASKING QUESTIONS

Asking the right questions will open the door to obtaining the full story from our client. It also conveys that you genuinely seek to understand what they are experiencing, their pain and their joy. Obviously, questions are important to gather the information you need to help the client accomplish their goals. Asking the right questions at the right time and in the right manner requires skill and practice and if done correctly, can be used during therapy sessions or in supervisory and training sessions.

You can use questions to lead the client to possible solutions, clarity, and insight. An invaluable tool in changing behavior is asking questions that foster greater awareness so that the client or trainee can better figure out the changes they need to make. Questions can indirectly prompt them to uncover information helping them determine a course of action for themselves.

There are many kinds of questions. Open-ended questions provide the opportunity for those you are working with to uncover a great deal of information in a more process-based manner, but they can be difficult to answer in a productive way. Answering open-ended questions requires that the client or trainee has enough understanding or enough insight to participate fully. Of course, you can always adjust your question based on the response you get, to help them better arrive at an answer that benefits them. Essentially you have to decide what level of prompt to provide; for an open-ended question to be effective, it should successfully guide the client to possible answers. And, as with all thoughtful prompts, as the client or trainee begins to answer questions in a more independent manner, they should be faded. The therapist should be thoughtful and systematic in how the question is posed.

Another kind of question to pose is one that is close-ended, typically answered by responding "yes" or "no" or another one word answer. For example, "Is it possible that you are afraid your husband will be upset if you give him honest feedback?" You can make the question range from being extremely easy to answer to quite difficult. You will need to gauge the difficulty of the question by how it may affect the process. Do they mind being wrong or is the answer too threatening?

You can ask multiple-choice questions. "Is the reason you don't provide feedback because you don't want your child to be upset, or you don't think it would be helpful?" This can evoke a little more thinking than true or false questions. And of course, you can provide more choices and alter the difficulty.

When asking questions, you don't want to sound like a quiz master or an interrogator. It can come across to the client as if you are testing them. Asking the wrong question or asking at the wrong time can make the client feel inadequate if they don't know the answer. So, before you ask a question you need to have a pretty good idea whether they know the answer. It is similar to when someone is lecturing and early in the presentation the speaker asks the audience a question. There is deafening silence because the audience doesn't have the necessary information to answer the question. It is not only uncomfortable for the audience, but it breaks momentum. Or perhaps even worse, someone gives an answer that is completely off the mark. Then you have to correct the person which makes them regret having spoken up and creates discomfort for all.

You should also be prepared for questions that clients and trainees will ask you. Recognize that there are many reasons why people ask questions. People don't necessarily ask questions because they want information. There are many other possible reasons:

- Reassurance that they are correct
- Comforting to hear the answer
- Refreshing their memory
- Fishing for a compliment
- Because they disagree with you
- For engagement
- As a prompt to change behavior

If they ask a question for which you don't know the answer, you may need a little time to process the question. So, you may ask them to repeat the question. Or ask for clarification. You can also paraphrase the question. If you are early in the relationship, admitting you don't know may erode the client's confidence so you can respond that it's a great question and that you want to think more about it and will get back to them later. Just make sure you do! Not only does it give you more time to think about it, but also offers an opportunity to get assistance if needed. However, later on in the relationship you can safely admit that you don't know the answer but will find it out.

ACTIVE LISTENING BLOCKERS

Similar to therapeutic alliance, there are some blockers to active listening. We have all experienced those people who clearly don't seem to care what you are saying. They barely, if at all, wait for a pause so that they can interject what they think or tell their story. When their response has nothing to do with what you said, it leaves the feeling that they are preoccupied with what they want to say and aren't really listening. Another sign of not being a good listener is not asking a follow-up question when one is clearly in order. The poor listener doesn't have a reaction to something that was tremendously personal or emotional to what you just revealed. Are they just insensitive or did they not listen? Once again, this all sounds so very obvious, but time and time again we see it's not obvious at all.

Consider the parent who reveals the tremendous pain they have felt regarding their child receiving a diagnosis of autism. A BCBA who is overly focused on developing a treatment plan for the child may fail to respond to the pain the parent just expressed. That is not being empathic nor compassionate. Just continuing with your own preset agenda leaves the parent out in the cold. Be careful that your own discomfort with the intense emotion being expressed by the parent does not cause you to skip over an important issue that requires validation. Amazingly we have seen instances where the BCBA ignores the response of the parent because they don't want to reinforce what they perceive to be a diversion from the real task or a play for sympathy. And if it's because they simply don't know what to say, that's a sign they haven't received proper clinical training.

ATTRIBUTES OF AN OUTSTANDING LISTENER

- It may start simply with body language. Look engaged, lean your body forward, use appropriate eye contact. Facial expressions are essential in showing that you are listening and interested. Be sure they are congruent with the tone and emotion of the conversation.

- Don't be too quick to interrupt! Give the speaker a chance to express their thoughts.

- When they are done, make sure that you truly understand what they said. Paraphrase to make sure you heard correctly and understand what is going on with them.

- Ask questions to clarify and continue the dialogue, not to interrupt or interject your opinion.

- Be prepared to gently slow down the process. Often when engaged in important conversations, people talk at lightning speed. You may miss important information or there may be too much information to process. Moreover, it doesn't give the client or trainee time to process. Often it will be necessary to guide and promote slowing down using both verbal and nonverbal prompts.

- Do everything humanly possible not to sound judgmental!

- Don't be too quick to enter the problem-solving phase. Of course, it is your job to make sure you get there, but it's a matter of timing. When you do get there, guard against defaulting to prescriptive mode as we will discuss in Chapter 7.

- At all costs, guard against discounting and instead aim for validation. All too often we hear BCBAs make statements that parents shouldn't feel sad or angry, or that their emotions are unfounded or an overreaction.

- Maintain compassion for the challenges that parents face just to get through the day. Don't be the person who gets impatient when parents don't follow your brilliant recommendations. We will cover this in Chapter 6.

References

Kolu, C. (2022, February). New 4h course: autism, TIBA, and ethics. *Cuspemergence.com.*
https://cuspemergence.com/2022/02/

LeBlanc, L.A., Taylor, B.A. & Marchese, N.V. (2020). The Training Experiences of Behavior Analysts: Compassionate
Care and Therapeutic Relationships with Caregivers. *Behavior Analysis Practice* 13, 387–393 https://doi.org/10.1007/
s40617-019-00368-z

Miller, M. (2021, June). *Compassionately assessing challenging behavior.* Invited presentation for Luna ABA. Online.

Poll everywhere. https://blog.polleverywhere.com/apply-active-listening-to-a-remote-team/
#:~:text=%E2%80%9CActive%20listening%20refers%20to%20a,and%20withholding%20judgment%20and%20advice

Rajaraman, A., Austin, J. L., Gover, H. C., Cammilleri, A. P., Donnelly, D. R., & Hanley, G. P. (2022). Toward trauma-
informed applications of behavior analysis. *Journal of Applied Behavior Analysis*, 55(1), 40-61.

Rogers, C.R., & Farson, R.E. (1957) *Active listening.* Chicago, IL: Industrial Relations Center of the University of Chicago.

Sadavoy, J. A., Zube, M. L. (2021). *A scientific framework for compassion and social justice: Lessons in Applied Behavior
Analysis.* Routledge. Abingdon, Oxfordshire.

Taylor, B. A., LeBlanc, L. A., & Nosik, M. R. (2018). Compassionate care in behavior analytic treatment: Can outcomes be
enhanced by attending to relationships with caregivers? *Behavior Analysis in Practice.* Advance online publication. doi:
10.1007/s40617-018-00289-3

CHAPTER 5

EXPECTATIONS & COLLABORATION

While the therapeutic alliance is essential in successful therapy and training outcomes, it is far more than just the positive relationships between the therapist/supervisor and client/trainee. Research has demonstrated that agreement on the focus of therapy/supervision, as well as the understanding of the process, is also essential. This results in an increased likelihood of achieving goals.

It begins with asking the client/trainee what they want to accomplish. What are their hopes? Fully explore this topic, not only what they want to accomplish, but why? Why will it enrich their life/career? The more information that you can gather, the more you will be able to help increase their motivation to engage in the process. Actively and respectfully listen. Ask questions to better understand their mission. For example:

Goal: To have better communication with your partner

Outcome: Will have a stronger relationship

Explore: How would that enhance your life? What does it mean to have a stronger relationship?

Goal: To increase prompting skill

Outcome: Will become a better teacher

Explore: How will that improve your professional outlook and the progress of your clients?

Encourage them to list several goals. Narrow their goals by finding commonalities across them (typically these commonalities are the fundamental skills from which many goals then blossom). Focus energy on those that you think are not only foundational to their overall success, but achievable. Beginning with achievable goals allows the trainee or client to experience success more quickly, sets the occasion for further reinforcement and buy-in with the process. For the clinician or supervisor, this may involve being a great shaper, skillfully leading them to select their optimal goal.

It is important they fully recognize that accomplishing the selected goals will be essential for their well-being. This will spark intrinsic motivation and thus buy-in. When clients or trainees are fully bought-in, they are inspired, and it's far easier to begin the tough work. Sometimes we will create a paradox: "Perhaps this will be a little too difficult. Perhaps it's not the right time." This causes them to protest and insist that they are fully committed. The more motivated they are, the more successful the process will be. If they are not fully charged and committed, it will come back to bite both of you at some point.

Throughout the process you will still need to inspire them to want to continue. Change is difficult. You will need to revisit the reason why *they* want to change, why accomplishing these goals will help them thrive. And so, when resistance occurs—and it will!—you can circle back and tap into their initial motivation to accomplish their goals.

It is equally essential that they fully understand the process (this will also be discussed in the chapter on the Autism Partnership Method [APM] supervision model): that it will be collaborative; that you will be providing guidance and information, but that they will be doing the heavy lifting; that they actually have the answers, it's simply your job to bring them to light. You will need to fully help them understand and embrace that it is indeed a process. It is not quick or linear. But anything worth doing is worth the investment. It will involve tons of challenges and mistakes, but it is indeed valuable and will be an amazing learning experience for both.

Establishing the goals and discussing the process is like the inspirational pep talk before the big game. Perhaps it's worth visiting YouTube and watching Knute Rockne in the locker room or Gene Hackman in *Hoosiers*! Pick examples and analogies that resonate with the client or trainee.

As discussed, motivation may flag from time to time. It may be due to the difficulty of accomplishing important change, and the fatigue that sets in when the process is taking longer than anticipated. You may need to help them recognize the progress that has occurred and inspire them to be reinforced by smaller steps toward a long-term goal. You may need to remind them of what made them eager at the outset and all the benefits that will accrue as a result of doing the work. Sometimes it's being Columbo (a detective in a drama series who was warm, polite and used the technique of acting confused to get to the heart of a case). Know when it's time to gently confront their lapses of follow through. Consider the following:

- Start with expressing your confusion with what is occurring

- Acknowledge that change is difficult

- Remind them of their goal and why they chose to pursue it

- Ask how you can best help

- Inquire if they want to continue with acquiring the goal or perhaps moving on to another one on the list

Example:

I am a little confused about how you are responding to your wife. It seems like when she discusses a problem that she is experiencing that you are going back to your habit of problem-solving. I fully understand that you are trying to help. But as we've discussed, she doesn't find it helpful and feels that you are being insensitive. I know that is absolutely not your intent. Nonetheless, it leads to both of you being angry and resentful. Ultimately, it has put a huge wedge in your marriage.

You have made great progress in being a better listener. However, recently it feels that you have gone back into your old pattern. Is that what you are experiencing, too? I'm wondering if it's just too hard to avoid problem-solving. Or that you have decided it's just not something you want to work on?

I know changing communication patterns is extremely difficult. And imagine you are frustrated with not helping despite knowing that it's detrimental to your relationship.

So, I am wondering how we should best proceed.

Example:

I know that your goal is to become a supervisor. You have said that being a supervisor will eventually result in you having incredible opportunities such as consulting around the country.

As we have discussed, to be able to achieve your objective, you will need to improve your critical thinking skills. And the way to improve will be through my providing honest feedback. I fully understand that it can be difficult to hear what you need to improve on.

It seems to me that you are upset when I do provide feedback. So, I'm perplexed about what to do. Perhaps I will stop providing constructive feedback. I do fear that this will slow the process, but I don't want to upset you. So, how should we proceed?

Your goal is that they regain their motivation to the process. Perhaps you even consider using a paradox. That is, you assert that perhaps you should put the process on hold or even terminate. It's risky, but can often be quite effective.

THE TAKEAWAY

When working with clients, parents or trainees, it is essential that you are working in collaboration. That you have the same agenda. That there are high expectations of success. It is important to establish this early on and revisit it throughout the process. As we have said repeatedly, change is difficult. Even when it's something in your best interest and something you truly desire.

CHAPTER 6

RESISTANCE

- the act of resisting, opposing or withstanding

- the opposition offered by one thing, force, etc. to another

- opposition to an attempt to bring repressed thoughts or feelings into consciousness

- the act of fighting against something that is attacking you, or refusing to accept something

- a refusal to go along with or accept from another

As we will discuss in more detail in **Chapter 7,** employing a psychoeducational approach typically involves not giving the answers or providing directive recommendations, not giving "the prescription." While there will be times when it makes sense to recommend a specific course of action or to provide a direct answer to a question, it is a slippery slope; resisting this temptation will pay great dividends in the long run. The goal is to have the client, parent, or trainee arrive at possible solutions and eventually, the best solution, as independently as possible. Put another way, the goal is to unobtrusively guide them to the process that solves their problem or begins to address it in a productive manner without you having to just "give them the answer."

This takes patience, foresight, active listening and an eye trained on the final goal, no matter where in the process the client or trainee is in that moment. It allows for stumbles and triumphs and learning from both. This is the process required for a greater development of an individual methodology, skill or style, with your oversight discreetly tucked away, unremarkable, inconspicuous. Ultimately, if a trainee, parent or client credit themselves in the development of their own process and recommendations, the more likely they will follow them. But even in the best of conditions, and even when following all the guidelines we have discussed up to this point, the path is by no means linear or completely free of difficulty and tribulation.

Despite your best efforts, anticipate that resistance is likely to occur at some point in the process. Even with initial all-around eagerness to participate in the process, there will be times of ambivalence and questioning whether the work on the goals is worth it. It's natural to be disappointed when this happens, but don't let it catch you off-guard. It is better to take these setbacks in progress as opportunities to advance understanding, recommit to the goal and then again move forward.

When resistance appears, the path forward becomes blocked: The trainee, client or parent is not following suggestions or recommendations when they are offered, or they are beginning to question outright the direction of therapy or whether they are getting benefit. They may even begin to falter in a course of action they have committed to on their own. There are times these blockages frustrate the therapist or catch them off-guard. Perhaps the therapist interprets these events personally or reacts to them in an emotional manner. We hear the word "resistant" used often to describe the behavior of the client or parent, and it carries a negative, confrontive connotation. Digging a bit deeper, the client's behavior may even be interpreted as noncompliance and turning their back on the therapist or supervisor. It is very human to react to resistance with consternation which can block consideration of where this resistance originates. It feels like one person must be on the correct path and the other person is not. Of course, as the therapist or supervisor our first instinct is we are right and the other person is obstinate, or lacks understanding. The therapist must engage in self-reflection, remain calm, and be objective. We can use our behavior analytic skills to identify the behavior and pursue uncovering its function. Rather than respond emotionally or in a dismissive manner, the therapist should ask, "Why is it happening?"

As a good behaviorist, the therapist should formulate alternative hypotheses. Consider all possible functions for this seemingly unexpected response. Before concluding there is "disagreement for disagreement's sake," check if that is truly the case. Ask questions, both of yourself and of the person appearing resistant. Perhaps you have misunderstood what was said. Rely on active listening and paraphrase what was heard. Clarify, have a constructive conversation, model compassion and the desire to better understand. Remain attentive but neutral, not evaluative or defensive.

What is commonly called "resistance" is typically complex and may be affected by variables not immediately obvious to the therapist. For example, it may include reticence or an apparent unwillingness to collaborate in the process. There can be agitation or displays of unease, or they may appear put off by the interactions or suggestions. Other indicators may be cancellations or avoidance of the process of therapy. Their actions may contradict what they state they believe or be inconsistent with what they have stated to be their goal. Assessing the function will allow the therapist to respond in an effective manner and get past the roadblock. If we misinterpret the function, the roadblock will still be there. Accurate assessment allows the therapist to determine the best course of action required to address why the "resistance" is happening, to be proactive and re-establish a collaborative, engaged relationship.

Probably the first hypothesis to consider is whether I am steering the ship in the wrong direction. As a therapist, it is important to be humble. Be able to recognize that even with the best of intentions, your recommendations may have missed the mark. If that is the case, you should own it. Learn from mistakes and grow. Demonstrate grace. The best way to handle this type of resistance is to admit they are part of the process and use these times to model how to handle feedback and correction. Nobody knows it all. And if you project as a "know-it-all" when you conduct therapy, that's a recipe for legitimate resistance. Keep in mind you may have been right in identifying a course of action that would have produced enormous benefit if it was correctly and sufficiently implemented. But that's a big "if..." There are valid reasons why that action was not taken. One reason why a brilliant plan might fail is that the person implementing it does not have the confidence and the foundational knowledge to be able to implement it correctly. A second reason is that you may have underestimated the amount of effort that is required to implement the plan. The best treatment plan is the one that the client or trainee can see themselves actually being able to implement. That might mean making a compromise that is less ambitious, but more likely to be consistently implemented.

A second possible reason for resistance could be erosion in the therapeutic connection. Has anything occurred that possibly changed the dynamic of the relationship? Perhaps you have come off as being judgmental? Has something you said been interpreted differently than what you meant? Have you been a good listener throughout the process? Has the client or trainee changed their perspective on the goals or the process? Have things changed in their life? Perhaps it's an indication that you are misaligned with them? You will have to determine if it is repairable. Sometimes resistance is simply an indication that your help is no longer appreciated or wanted, and the client has decided to move on with their life. In that case we should plan a strategy that allows a graceful pause in the work, or assist the client in finding a person that is a better match for them.

Here are some examples of the many forms of resistance and responses that take into account the possible function(s) of the resistance:

They didn't understand the recommendation; there is confusion or a lack of knowledge.	Review your recommendations and use different language and examples. As always, frame them from the client's perspective.
There is indifference or a lack of engagement with the recommendation.	If your objectives don't align with theirs, have a deeper conversation about priorities, focus on the commonalities.
They are in favor of the process but terrified of acting upon it.	Slow the process, listen actively, work on building expertise and confidence. Break skills down, support the journey.
They appear aloof or somehow "wronged."	Perhaps you have slighted them or misjudged their expertise; discuss further and review active listening.
They appear jaded, or they have "heard it all before;" or there is a displaced anger/resentment seething due to past professional experiences.	Perhaps they have a history of intervention not going well, or feeling they were not a meaningful participant in the process. Rebuild trust, share experiences, listen to their grievances.

They appear scattered, chaotic or disorganized at the thought of implementing recommendations or continuing the process.	Consider focusing on stress management and coping or organizing the material and the process in a more digestible manner. Break skills down, reprioritize, work on their confidence and follow-through.
There is lack of follow-through, or not wanting to deal with the hassle it all entails.	Rediscover meaningful rationales for the continuation of therapy, individualize the reasons for continuing the journey so it matches their hopes.
Not resistance but actually hopelessness.	"It's never worked before." Explain differences, listen to the experiences, empathize, tailor to include areas they contribute to the process. Identify some small easier steps that might provide an early feeling of success and engender hope.
The proposed change seems overwhelming.	Fully acknowledge that change can be difficult. Discuss the process of change. Perhaps teaching stress management is in order to cope with the anxiety of changing. Also consider baby steps. Share with them that with time it will become easier and ultimately help them reach their goals.
It is philosophically different from their belief system.	Get to better understand their perspectives and how it may actually work within their belief system. You may need to reframe the recommendations so they are more congruent with their belief system. Find commonalities, areas of shared belief to rebuild connectedness and rapport.
They may like the recommendation, but they are completely overwhelmed so trying something new is more than they can currently handle.	Fully acknowledge the difficulty of their situation and perhaps consider reprioritizing or taking baby steps or revisiting it at a later time.

It may be a recommendation they like but their partner or family doesn't agree. Therefore, they are in a predicament.	Fully discuss and assist with problem-solving. Zero in on the components that the client can more fully control.
Not being resistant, just not their priority.	Re-examine your understanding of their priorities. Determine if there are still areas to address that are important to them.
Consider that their rejection is because you haven't addressed the root issue. Thus, their resistance is because it doesn't actually address the issue.	Dive deeper, try to figure out what you have missed.
Perhaps they have a habit of automatically rejecting ideas or change; they come across as oppositional.	Share your observations and explore how aware they are of this automatic response. See if they are agreeable to targeting that behavior. Give honest feedback. Look for opportunities to reinforce them when they respond with more openness. Explore any feelings of discouragement that undermine their motivation. Remind each other of times when being courageous has led to a positive outcome.

Resistance and all its potential functions is in fact a wonderful opportunity to reset the process, to reevaluate and to reflect. Moreover, when you hit a roadblock, it is often an indication that you have actually uncovered a critical issue. Perhaps *the* issue. It is similar to when a client's eyes well up with tears; you know you have hit close to home. When these moments present themselves, you don't want to avoid uncomfortable situations. Often that would be colluding with the client or trainee by not addressing the important issues. We should facilitate the client maintaining contact with the uncomfortable material so that the discomfort can extinguish. We may have to nudge them compassionately and provide rationales to them so that they understand the discomfort will diminish over time if they don't keep running away from it.

Often when it seems that we are on different pages, in reality we may be closer than it appears. Try to figure out where indeed there is agreement. If you take note of the examples of possible functions of "resistance," you may notice there are amazing opportunities to dive deeper, and work through roadblocks that the client was not aware of. Typically, we all want the same terminal goal, and we can find fertile common ground if we only spend enough time with the process. We might need to backtrack and take a different fork in the road in order to get to the destination.

Finally, we should always keep in mind what we can do to prevent resistance and keep the process moving forward. Here are key steps to preventing and working through resistance:

- Be diligent in active listening and conveyance of empathy. Make sure you fully understand their perspective. Before concluding that they are resistant, make sure that you have fully immersed yourself in walking a mile in their shoes.

- Find as much common ground as possible between your apparently discrepant viewpoints and maintain the emphasis on areas of agreement. That can diminish the apparent size of the disagreement.

- If it's in your style, using humor can be helpful. Of course, be sure it's not demeaning in any way and be sure it does not distract from the process. It can be an effective way to defuse emotional tension.

- Share those things you find valuable and meaningful in the other person's emotional expressions, whether it is joyful or has a negative edge. Frustration, anger, and disillusionment can provide a source of motivation to do good. Emotion is nothing to shy from.

- Don't rush the process. Slow down, take baby steps.

- Periodically (and proactively) revisit goals and recommit to vision of how the process is expected to flow. Maintain buy-in!

- *"You can't need or want it more than the client."* This was sage advice from Marilyn. If you can't inspire them to thirst for change, that will become an insurmountable obstacle.

- Make sure your expectations are achievable, applicable and appropriate.

- It has been said that when there is resistance, you are also resisting the client's position. Could it also be your issue? It's another area of possible function to explore, particularly in your own therapy or overlaps with your mentor.

THE TAKEAWAY

When you encounter resistance take that as a reminder that there is a mismatch in expectations. Take a deep breath. Don't blame the client or the trainee. Carefully analyze why they are not accepting recommendations and identify what course corrections are necessary. You will either need to alter the goal, plan smaller steps or increase the motivation. Probably all three.

CHAPTER 7

SOME CURRENT DIMENSIONS OF ABA CLINICAL SUPERVISION

RON LEAF & JONATHAN RAFUSE

During the delivery of behavioral treatment services for children with autism, there are many identified factors which impact the outcome. Research has shown that treatment intensity (dosage), early introduction of treatment, and severity of autism symptoms will have a powerful impact on how rapidly a child progresses (Ala'i-Rosales & Zeug, 2010; Ben-Itzchak & Zachor, 2007; Dixon et al., 2016; Eldevik et al., 2009; Fenske et al., 1985; Harris & Handleman, 2000). Some of those factors we can control, some we cannot. At the top of our list of what we should endeavor to control is the skill set of interventionists. Therefore, the initial training and ongoing supervision a trainee receives is central to ensuring maximum outcomes for our clients.

Over the decades of our clinical work, we have come to see the value of a progressive approach to the science of ABA (Leaf et al., 2017; Leaf et al., 2016; Leaf et al., 2011; Lovaas, 1987), and we strive to apply a progressive framework to supervision. At the core of our supervision delivery are several dimensions that we believe will contribute to the formation of highly skilled and effective interventionists. These dimensions include: (a) setting the right expectations, (b) willingness to allow mistakes, (c) balancing positive and corrective feedback, (d) timeliness of feedback, (e) level of directiveness, (f) clinical judgment and critical thinking, (g) focus on client vs. trainee, and (h) intensity. These dimensions are foundational to comprehensive supervision, and this chapter is devoted to both their description and the considerations of when and how to apply them to achieve the best possible outcomes.

DEFINING THE SUPERVISORY RELATIONSHIP

Just as building a strong therapeutic alliance between interventionist and client is crucial to a successful psychotherapy outcome, so is establishing a supervision alliance between the trainer and trainee for ABA. This entails collaborative agreement on goals to be accomplished, methods that will be employed, the expectations of both parties (i.e., the work to be done), and a plan for sustaining motivation (i.e., the reinforcers) through a long-term mutual endeavor. This alliance is critical to successful supervision outcome.

A good place to begin is having the "talk." This talk may include some uncomfortable reality checks. Both parties need to enter this professional relationship with eyes wide open. The initial talk lays the foundation for buy-in to the process and sets the stage for ongoing collaboration and growth. During ongoing conversations, you will revisit the objectives to evaluate what has been accomplished and how well the process is working, make adjustments to the format, and update the goals. Let's put this in context with other kinds of talks that are influential in promoting personal and professional growth and successful relationships.

In life we experience many memorable talks, transformative due to the information they impart and the self-inquiry that is inspired. One example may be the talk parents and their children have regarding sexuality. Often parents go into this talk with trepidation. For some families, it ushers in a new, complicated element defining the relationship. It can shape how further conversation will occur, or not occur. Is everyone comfortable with the subject? Will there be receptiveness? Is the timing right? Are the parents at ease with their own history, their memories of this talk with their parents? It's a fraught topic to broach, but so important in the child's understanding of themselves and influential in how they engage in future relationships.

Another example is talks within an intimate relationship. Perhaps you must reveal something difficult, that is uncomfortable to share, and you anticipate will be uncomfortable to hear. It can be about divergent opinions and beliefs and how to find common ground. It can be about how you are experiencing each other and the relationship. Are we on the same page? Will we be able to move forward? Or do we cut our losses and say goodbye?

In the clinical world of autism treatment, the talk may refer to parents discussing their child's diagnosis with the child, family members or a friend. Do we reveal it or not? When is the right time? How will the information be received? Is it best for the child to know? (We believe it is.)

These examples of momentous talks have shared characteristics. They are potentially difficult to begin and may cause discomfort in the short term. But they also impart important information and are worth every moment. Important talks are best approached with sensitivity, patience and comfort with the content and delivery. It is critical to have a clear vision of both the immediate goals and how those translate to future aspirations. This is also the case with the talk occurring between supervisors and trainees.

CONCEPTUALIZING SUPERVISORY TALKS

Supervisory talks benefit the trainee by helping establish realistic short- and long-term goals. They are the forum for clarifying expectations about how the process will unfold, inoculating trainees against the potential trials and tribulations that they will encounter along the way, and establishing the precedent for receiving honest feedback.

Setting Goals. The talks should be inspiring and pragmatic. They can be presented as a series of Teaching Interaction Procedures (TIPs; Leaf et al., 2009; Phillips et al., 1971, 1974). First, the skill set is identified; e.g., "We will be working on the skills necessary for you to become a strong, independent clinician." Then meaningful rationales are developed for participating in this intensive process. Mutually brainstorm the goals to be accomplished. Then start honing the list: which goals are considered priorities? Which goals may accomplish more than one objective, making the list more efficient? The supervisor shapes the trainee's desires into realistic, clearly defined objectives. It provides a road map for becoming a fully competent clinician.

For example, a trainee may aspire to "become a consultant working with school districts." This may be reasonable, but part of the supervisor's role at this point is to temper the enthusiasm with consideration of a realistic path toward accomplishing that goal. Breaking this goal down into achievable components and providing a realistic timeframe can be incorporated into the TIP. Being a consultant working with school districts requires considerable skill development combining numerous short-term steps finally leading to that ultimate goal. This could potentially take years of experience. But if the supervisor practices active listening, presents with confidence and helps the trainee see the path the supervision process will follow to attain that goal, the result is encouragement of what is eventually achievable rather than discouragement. Being honest is essential and colluding with an unrealistic timeframe would sooner or later undermine the process. We can see here the importance of powerful rationales.

The next step in the TIP would be for the trainee to practice the skill. If they have been paying attention, then they know what to do. They tackle the next goal they hope to accomplish in the supervision process, define it clearly and then break it down into achievable component skills. When used correctly, TIPs are effective, efficient and above all, collaborative. Powerful, individualized reinforcement is established early in the process and repeated practice leads to greater proficiency and, ultimately, greater independence.

For the invested trainee, maintaining patience can be a challenge. Establishing achievable goals and a realistic timeframe early in the supervisory relationship is critical. These goals may evolve over time, or some goals may be replaced with others as the supervision process continues. It is important to be flexible within the basic supervision plan to allow for the best training outcome.

EXPECTATIONS FOR FEEDBACK

Promoting a trainee's clinical skill requires them practicing technique for thousands of hours and receiving feedback—lots of feedback! Studies have clearly supported two conditions contributing to best outcomes: 1) the ability to learn from reinforcement *and* corrective feedback; 2) thinning reinforcement to the most natural, intermittent schedule (e.g., Stokes & Baer, 1977).

Too much praise! There is such a thing as too much praise. An unjustifiably rich reinforcement schedule is unrealistic, unsustainable, difficult to fade, and completely unfair to the trainee. Being compassionate in this case means providing the trainee with honest feedback. To hamstring supervision by taking away one of its most effective training tools only sets the staff up for failure.

Praise should be contingent and commensurate with the quality of the behavior it follows. While it makes sense to ensure that the supervision experience is reinforcing, that does not mean that praise should be gratuitous. This is not a little league where everyone gets the same trophy. As a form of feedback, praise is only effective to the extent that it is accurate and honest. If a supervisor simply wants to keep the trainee happy, that is disingenuous; training with this purpose does not prepare a trainee for the reality beyond the training sessions. It is not sustainable, and the result is a less skilled interventionist and potentially a feeling of betrayal. Additionally, we must not assume that praise is a reinforcer. Not everyone likes praise, and not everyone is motivated by receiving a prize when there is no challenge involved.

Sandwich, Anyone? "Sandwiching" is a style of delivering a combination of corrective feedback and praise during a debrief. Typically, the supervisor starts with positive feedback, then offers corrective feedback, then ends with another positive. If this were a sandwich, it would be two pieces of white bread with nothing but sauerkraut between the slices. It is designed to take the "sting" out of corrective feedback, but can come across as disingenuous. This delivery method makes corrective feedback appear completely negative, something to hide. Often trainees don't even pay attention to the praise because they know the real message is in the middle. This method diminishes the praise and demonizes the corrective feedback. Or the alternative, equally undesirable, effect is the trainee doesn't effectively hear the corrective feedback because it has been hidden between two fluffy pieces of praise. Either way, "sandwiching" defeats the purpose of both reinforcement and corrective feedback. Possibly worse, it exposes the supervisor's discomfort with giving straightforward, honest, and necessary constructive feedback. This could erode credibility and damage the supervisory relationship. A simple solution may be to provide commentary in the order in which events unfolded and provide reinforcement or correction as deserved.

THE ROLE OF CORRECTIVE FEEDBACK

Corrective feedback is a critical component of the learning process, whether given to a client in a discrete trial teaching session, or to a trainee accumulating examples and non-examples of a targeted skill. Corrective feedback should be crafted in a way to guide the trainee on what to do differently, in a manner they comprehend with the opportunity to immediately practice the better version of the skill. Corrective feedback does not have to be aversive; it should be informational and delivered in a calm, nonjudgmental manner. It should be seen as a normal component of a supervision session, highlighting what to change to move towards greater proficiency.

At the outset of the supervisory process, trainees may have little experience with receiving corrective feedback. They may not understand that it is a normal and essential part of professional development and is an opportunity to learn what to do differently, to achieve their professional goals. Remember, part of an initial supervisory talk should include inoculation, a clear explanation of what and how corrective feedback is and rationales for its use. The supervisor must develop ways to deliver feedback so that it is not received or interpreted personally. It needs to be framed and delivered in a manner that encourages comprehension, acceptance and the notion that this is but a tool to stimulate improvement.

An optimal response to feedback is to solidify the aspects of the trainee's performance that represent best practice and make corrections in implementation where needed. It should lead to better intervention, stronger understanding, and greater confidence. It should be concise and clear, and allow for a systematic, efficient fade to promote more independent application from the trainee. Rather than experiencing it as traumatic, the trainee will contact greater success and be sold on the value of honest feedback.

Not everyone is equally prepared to hear corrective feedback and is able to use it constructively. It may require desensitization by initially giving a lower dose of correction that elicits a milder emotional response. It gives the trainee the opportunity to feel a modicum of discomfort, and still be able to respond constructively. We can inoculate trainees by providing rationales. This may be as simple as statements like: "Mistakes will happen, and they are an opportunity to grow;" or "I will provide you unvarnished feedback; sugarcoating only obscures the message."

We have all been in the position of having the best laid plans for how to approach a session get completely derailed by unanticipated behavior from the client. As we know, clients sometimes don't follow our script. The trainee will undoubtedly make many mistakes, even with careful forethought. Helping the trainee understand that mistakes will happen goes a long way toward promoting a more realistic view of the supervisory process.

Working through those challenges will make the trainee a better clinician. If the supervisor has sufficiently inoculated the trainee, and then facilitated the trainee practicing the skill set necessary to dig themself out of a hole they've created, mistakes become incredible growth opportunities.

CORRECTION CONSIDERATIONS

A compassionate supervisor knows that corrective feedback during supervision can be truly tough to hear. The greatest impediment to the use of corrective feedback is that it can be received personally, as a reflection of inadequacy, or in some way demeaning. Sometimes this can be a result of how the trainee experiences correction. But other times, it can be due to the supervisor's poor delivery. Supervisors are on a training path of their own, and they possibly require guidance and practice when providing corrective feedback, ideally away from their trainees. How corrective feedback is delivered and how it is received is important. If not addressed, both the lack of this clinical skill in supervisors and the lack of perspective in trainees can be a supervision blocker.

Timing. Another important element of the supervisor's decision-making is the timing of feedback. The question the supervisor must answer is whether to provide feedback in the moment as ABA intervention is occurring, or at a later time? We have found that the answer is "it depends." The considerations about timing include: urgency of correcting the trainee's course of action; how developed are the trainee's skills and where they are in the supervisory process; and what will propel them the farthest in the attainment of their short- and long-term goals.

Our primary concern is the safety and well-being of both our clientele and our staff. This precedes any other consideration in our profession. So, if in the course of treatment, or if in the course of training, a client or staff member is in danger, then the supervisor should calmly and assertively intervene by whatever means necessary to address the issue as discreetly as possible. There is a range of responses for the supervisor's corrective intervention, but basic behavioral guidelines suggest it occur as unobtrusively as possible, with minimal attention to interfering behavior and all attention on the safety of the client and trainee.

This may include stopping the session, having the supervisor temporarily step in or immediately suggesting a course of action to remedy the situation. Once the crisis is resolved, the supervisor should debrief with the trainee. This should occur as soon as possible, but only after the excitement or adrenaline has faded and the trainee is calm and receptive. Then the supervisor can provide feedback and offer insight promoting a better outcome if the situation occurs again. Another reason to consider intervening in the moment would be if the actions of the trainee would inadvertently promote an undesired behavior pattern that could be difficult to undo, or if they are acting in a manner that is disrespectful of the client.

Apart from concerns about safety and protecting the dignity of the client, sometimes the decision to correct immediately or delay delivery depends on where the trainee is in the training process. Early on, a trainee may lack the knowledge or experience needed to work their way out of adversity during a treatment session. This is a time to provide feedback as soon as something requires correction. And since supervision relies on behavioral methodology, we can borrow from prompting guidelines: use the least intrusive correction that will still result in the needed behavior change. In this case, more immediate correction is analogous to a more assistive prompt that is more likely to obtain the desired result. Similarly, if the trainee is failing to learn from delayed feedback, then we should adjust the timing to be more optimal and reduce the risk of them continuing to repeat the error. More immediate feedback may bring the trainee more quickly to insight and in contact with reinforcement, which increases the likelihood they will make similar needed adjustments in the future.

Generally, though, supervisor input away from distractions and the intensity of ABA intervention sessions is preferable. Supervision during treatment sessions has many disadvantages when considering trainee comprehension. First, expecting the trainee to attend to the supervisor while delivering intervention is a difficult ask. The trainee should be focused on the treatment and the client. Think back to the sports analogy of coaching. The best coaches, no matter what age group or skill level, do not shout instructions during a game. In some sports, they cannot call "time-out" to give a player corrective feedback. Feedback will occur at halftime, the next day on the practice field, or in the screening room as the game is reviewed under less distracting conditions. A masterful teacher and coach, John Wooden, shared that he rarely coached during games, but saved that for practice.

Feedback Specificity. Another dimension of feedback is the degree of specificity. Again, the rule of thumb is don't be more specific than you need to. Try to make the trainee as accountable as possible for recognizing the mistake and how to correct it. If the trainee has progressed to being more independently analytic it might be sufficient to say, "Remember your target." If not, then it might be necessary to be more specific, e.g., "That is worth two tokens." It would be a sign of progress if you only had to say, "Be careful," and the trainee would remember that moment for later discussion. The admonition may not actually be an indication that the trainee needs to make an adjustment, but simply to ensure that they are aware of the risk they are taking, e.g., when a reinforcement schedule becomes very thin. The outcome of decisions made in these moments will influence both how the corrective feedback is received and how to effectively fade it, so the trainee is more self-reliant.

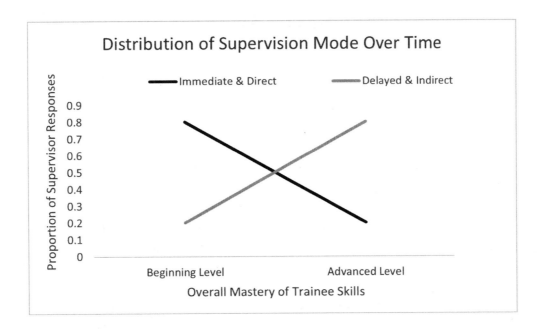

As the supervision process moves past the beginning stages, there should be observable growth in the skill set of the trainee. This brings the in-the-moment vs. delayed corrective feedback decision into sharper focus. If we consider all the possible input we can provide to trainees, it may help to visualize how the type of input varies over time. Here is a hypothetical graph that shows how the distribution of supervisor responses might change over time.

In the early stages of training, the proportion of supervision responses that are immediate and direct is higher. Over time, as the trainee's skills progress, we see the proportion of immediate and direct responses decline and responses that are delayed and indirect become the primary mode of supervision. The dimensions of immediacy and directiveness should be thought of as a continuum, and the supervisor is continually aiming for the optimal point along the continuum, according to the trainee's ability to profit from more opportunity to figure it out on their own, and decreased dependence on being told right away what needs to be changed. This is similar to the coach of a basketball player who is aiming to minimize input to the player in the middle of play, preferably using a limited number of time outs and the period breaks to discuss adjustments without disrupting the flow of the game. The lion's share of coaching takes place in post-game debriefing and pre-game preparation. In the delivery of behavioral health services, we need to take it a giant step farther because most of the game play occurs without the coach present.

Therefore, becoming your own coach is essential. If the supervisor is active during a session, they will not get an accurate picture of what happens when the supervisor is not present. The less the supervisor is involved in the decision-making process of the trainee, the better; the more they rely upon themself and the clinical skills the supervision has helped develop (i.e., in-the-moment assessment, clinical judgment, technical expertise, curricular knowledge, clinical sensitivity, masterful reinforcement delivery and development, etc.), the better.

DEVELOPING CRITICAL THINKING AND BUILDING CLINICAL JUDGMENT

This framework for ongoing supervision offers opportunities for intensive teaching. "Intensive" as used here has a compound meaning: the focus and process of training is concentrated, the skill set is expansive, the time to achieve goals is open-ended, and the effort required is rigorous. The supervisor and trainee require determination and resolve, to say the least. Periodic inventory of goals that have been accomplished, can help maintain the motivation to sustain the quest for long-term goals, like becoming a consultant. Milestones along the way might include a broader repertoire of specific teaching strategies, progressing from individual instruction to group instruction, broader experience with a variety of clients, or a more in-depth knowledge of the scientific literature. Together, the supervisor and supervisee are building the skill set we call clinical judgment.

Clinical judgment is the culmination of theoretical knowledge and application experience. It guides the trainee in moment-by-moment decision-making based on the synthesis of a broad range of variables that affect behavioral performance. This skill set depends on the trainee's ability to use critical thinking: the objective evaluation of data informing a decision.

Clinical judgment includes many components:

- Expertise in ABA-based teaching strategies, such as discrete trial teaching, the teaching interaction procedure, systematic desensitization, reinforcer development, and shaping

- A working knowledge of the foundations of ABA

- Keen observational skills

- Healthy skepticism and critical thinking

- A comprehensive understanding of the population being served

- Behavioral artistry

A major goal in supervision is increasing the trainee's ability to quickly synthesize information and be as responsive as possible to the performance of the client. As a starting point, the supervisor can arrange opportunities for the trainee to observe another person engaged in instruction with a client, either live or recorded. They should describe in as much detail as possible the most relevant variables that are influencing the client's responding during instruction. Using this information, they should then report what action they would take next and the rationale for that decision. The trainee can benefit equally from observing a novice instructor as well as an experienced instructor. This provides the opportunity to discriminate between mistakes and best practice. As they continue to observe instruction, the trainee assesses whether the client's subsequent behavior is consistent with the hypothesis they formulated, and revises their action plan accordingly. As the trainee becomes more fluent with the process, they will progress to carrying out all the steps while engaged in instruction with a client.

Remember the visualized line representing the range of supervisor input and its impact on skill generalization. The supervisor provides reinforcement, correction, and guidance in the manner and at the time most benefiting the trainee, depending on where they are on the continuum of skill development. As the trainee progresses through the supervisory framework, answers are provided less and less by the supervisor and are instead reached by the trainee applying their analytic skills.

In other professions this is the norm and is effective in developing proficiency. For example, consider the football ("soccer" to the uninitiated) academies designed to operate under these premises. Novice players are selected because of the promise they show on the field, typically at a young age. Once at the academy, they are immersed in all things football, including analysis, history, tactics, fitness, nutrition, endurance, and hours upon hours of application on the field of play. They are inoculated to learning under intense conditions, with supervision from coaches, physicians, nutritionists, educators and advanced level players. It may take years before the player graduates from intramural scrimmages to traveling B teams to eventually playing against international opponents. The progression occurs because of the mix of feedback, skill practice, education, and application. Reinforcement in the form of praise may be sparing, but the resulting confidence, tactical knowledge and technical skill exemplifies an expert positional player.

As the supervisory framework produces more trainee confidence and skill, the supervisor should refrain from providing answers and instead shape and encourage the trainee to rely on their own experience to do so. The supervisor guides trainees to ask the right questions and come to the answers themselves. To borrow from a saying, the supervisor is teaching the trainee to fish.

THE RANGE OF SUPERVISION DELIVERY

If the supervisor has developed a strong supervision process, then there is continual referencing of the training goals and where to operate along the continuum of direct vs. indirect guidance. Both the supervisor and the trainee are committed to continuing along the path to greater competence, confidence and greater autonomy during ABA treatment sessions. That path has definable methods for delivering pertinent information, and range from "most assistive" on one end to "least assistive" on the other, and a full range of delivery options in between. In this representation, the application of supervision should move along the continuum toward the least assistive methods promoting the trainee's skill acquisition.

MOST ASSISTIVE DELIVERY: PRESCRIPTIVE METHODOLOGY

The most assistive end of the supervision continuum is comprised of "prescriptive" delivery methods, just like going to the doctor when you are ill and they tell you exactly what remedy to take, how much of it, and when to take it. This end of the range allows for essential information to be delivered immediately, and the trainee is then able to implement the right procedure in the current situation. In the earliest stages of supervision, a prescriptive approach allows the trainee to be more successful from the outset. As with the whole supervision framework, prescriptive delivery should be used thoughtfully, with full awareness of the advantages and disadvantages.

For example, if the client is in crisis and the circumstances do not allow for the trainee to navigate out of the situation (e.g., the crisis is beyond the trainee's experience; the behaviors have become a safety concern for either the client or the trainee; the trainee is beyond what their skill level can remedy), then the supervisor should step in and provide support. The delivery could also be more prescriptive during initial training sessions, in which case the supervisor may incorporate brief narration with rationale to promote clearer understanding of the training objective. This type of supervision is aimed at quickly producing the correct performance, reducing errors and maximizing the time that the trainee spends practicing the skill correctly.

Initially, one of the goals of supervision may be to develop the trainee's comprehensive knowledge base. Knowing the principles behind effective ABA technique, having a firm grasp of behavior theory and developing treatment session preparedness may best be promoted through a straightforward didactic delivery method. This often is not the best time to rely upon a Socratic approach; the trainee may not have acquired the prerequisite knowledge and it would be extremely inefficient to force them to re-invent the wheel. As quickly as possible, we incorporate rationales and overarching principles so that we are building a framework for the trainee, eventually writing their own prescription.

Supervision provided in a more prescriptive manner has the advantage of promoting fluency in specific technical areas foundational to the practitioner's overall clinical development. This end of the continuum is represented by straightforward, fact- and rationale-based information being provided to the trainee. This supervision delivery is more assistive, more prescriptive, and completely distinguishable from the delivery that happens later in the process, where more independent "figuring it out" is encouraged.

Caution! Trainees will likely find a prescriptive approach to supervision to be very comfortable. If done correctly, the trainee is quickly successful as the given information is applied. That experience builds comfort and confidence with feedback and fosters buy-in to the whole process. However, it is essential for the supervisor to continually expand the comfort zone or both of you will get stuck there. As skills are learned and mastered, the supervisor should pull back and be less assistive. Relying upon more prescriptive delivery options for too long will erode the supervisory relationship and have a negative impact upon the overall mission.

When a trainee is further along in the supervision process and experiences challenges, a supervisor may naturally want to continue this mode of being supportive and intervening quickly. Quick fixes are a pitfall because they provide a sense of relief for the trainee and gratification for the supervisor. On the surface it feels supportive but it short circuits the discovery process for the trainee.

Becoming slower to give input and less definitive with a specific course of action allows more opportunity for the trainee to advance their assessment skills, critical thinking, and ability to figure it out on their own, even if it means more mistakes. This is where they become more independent in decision-making and refine their clinical judgment. The supervision has to systematically move towards less assistance and more independence as the trainee shows proficiency. Any temporary discomfort is outweighed by experiencing that they *can* figure it out for themself, and this ultimately builds confidence. Beware of the seductiveness of prescriptive quick fixes, as it can too easily become the default strategy.

Getting stuck in prescriptive mode is detrimental to the trainee's professional development. Even when sound rationales are provided along with the prescription, we can't be sure that trainees are actually internalizing the analytic considerations. Without completely understanding the specifics of why a certain recommendation is only applicable in the current situation, a trainee may overgeneralize the advice. If the advice sometimes works and sometimes does not, this can cause confusion. They will not be successful, and will end up retreating back to their comfort zone. Consider, too, that the trainee might come up with a better solution if the supervisor does not preempt that by too quickly telling them what to do. That's how great new ideas emerge in the development of our science: a newcomer thinks of a new way to do something that the old-timers never thought of.

If we view supervision methods as located along a continuum, then the supervisor should always strive to move towards a less assistive mode to promote professional growth. The supervisor and trainee must remember the long-term objectives: greater proficiency, greater confidence and greater independence, which only come with the fading of support. Prescriptive methods of supervision delivery have their place and time but should be used less and less as the supervision process continues.

LESS ASSISTIVE DELIVERY: THE PSYCHOEDUCATIONAL METHOD

At the less assistive end of the supervision continuum is the psychoeducational method. The psychoeducational approach encourages trainees to discover information for themselves, and to arrive more independently at insight. The trainee relies less on direction from the supervisor and more upon themself, the knowledge base that has been developed, and the use of critical thinking to maximally promote professional development. This movement towards greater independence is reliant on both supervisor skill and on trainee attainment of milestones established during the course of supervision. Shifting from more assistance to less requires planning, patience, empathy and a clear understanding of how and why the supervision is changing. If not addressed through the ongoing supervisory talks, this could be experienced as a loss of support. So, be sure to take the time to inoculate and prepare the trainee.

In the psychoeducational approach, the trainee's questions are not automatically provided with direct answers; there is not a presumption that we should give step-by-step instructions or immediate help when concerns arise during ABA treatment. They are instead guided through decision-making considerations, formulating the right questions to ask of themselves as they implement intervention, and then work through possible answers on their own. Typically, trainees develop hypotheses and practice articulating them. Then the hypotheses are tested in practice to accumulate evidence to support or revise the hypotheses. Collaboration and discussion around the process of finding answers predominates the supervisory sessions. Through exposure, without being rescued, they become increasingly comfortable with uncertainty. The *quest* for answers becomes reinforcing rather than just being handed the answer. Throughout this process, the supervisor uses behavioral methods. The supervisor is shaping better technique, more independent application and greater confidence in the procedures. The supervisory skill needed is assessment of where the trainee is in the process. Corrective feedback must be at the right dosage to both help the trainee arrive at insight and be as unobtrusive as possible. This is a dynamic process, with both supervisor and trainee actively involved in finding a supervision course that is optimal. As the trainee develops more skill proficiency, the supervisor continues to fade assistance.

Supervisor be aware! There are many variables that may lead to the supervision process breaking down or faltering as this process evolves. If not properly inoculated, the trainee may find the evolution of supervisory method difficult. But this is necessary; as the supervisor fades assistance, the responsibility for the intervention falls more squarely upon the shoulders of the trainee. Another pitfall may have to do with the client involved in the process. If supervision is exclusively focused on the immediate progress of the client, it may preclude allowing leeway for mistakes. Trainees need to be able to make mistakes and learn from them, and they can do so without jeopardizing the client's progress. Increasing the trainee's ability to operate independently will actually increase the long-term benefit to the client. Watching trainees make mistakes, fumble and get frustrated can be an uncomfortable experience. And unfortunately, some discomfort is inherent in the supervisor allowing the mistakes to happen to bolster the problem-solving skills of the trainee. These issues all contribute to the risk of flagging motivation or dissatisfaction with the process.

Secondly, when trainees ask questions, analyze. What is the purpose of the question? Is the trainee asking for information? Is it a challenge, or a reflection of dissatisfaction? Determining why a question is being asked will guide the supervisor in how to best answer it. Sometimes the supervisor won't know the answer to a question! Sometimes saying, "I don't know," is both the hardest and the most appropriate response to offer a trainee. But don't leave that lack of knowledge hanging in the air. Use this moment to model professionalism, find out the answer and provide it: "That was a great question, and I don't have a good answer right now. But I am going to tap some resources and get back to you so we can discuss it, practice it and learn from it."

Finally, implementing a more psychoeducational model for the delivery of supervision is just hard, requiring increased effort for all involved in the process. Implementation requires patience and confidence—an understanding that the long-term goals will be more effectively addressed, even though it can feel otherwise. As we said before, short-term pain for long-term gain. Leading trainees toward insight is difficult. Done incorrectly, the supervisor can sound like a quiz master, someone knowing the answers but malevolently withholding them from the trainee. This delivery methodology is not simply about asking questions of the trainee. It is not meant to be an inquisition or interrogation, but to the trainee, if this method is not done with clinical sensitivity, it can feel like it. Leading staff to ask themselves "how" questions and then articulate the answer, as well as "why" questions leading to articulation of the rationales for their decisions is not easy. As the relationship continues to evolve, as the trainee is reminded to embrace the process, and as trust and comfort settle in, this will become far easier. This process will eventually lead to a more informed and confident discussion and a more insightful and effective ABA interventionist. Like most goals in life, the effort is worth it, resulting in a trusted skill set for the trainee to rely on.

SUPERVISION BLOCKERS

The supervisor must be vigilant and engaged throughout the process. As with any dynamic relationship, there will be peaks and valleys. But being aware of potential supervision blockers will ensure the relationship does not completely break down. We already mentioned the pitfalls associated with the delivery and acceptance of corrective feedback. There are other blockers that can negatively impact the relationship: loss of motivation from the trainee, fear of mistakes, corrective feedback received as an affront, and ineffectual supervision. If these and other potential blockers are not recognized and addressed, the training could be compromised.

WANING MOTIVATION

The supervisor should always be aware of flagging morale or diminished motivation. This can present itself as disengagement, lack of enthusiasm, or argumentativeness. The trainee may begin to overuse mastered programming, requiring little effort from either interventionist or client during ABA treatment sessions. It can be a reluctance or avoidance of challenges in situations where there is a higher risk of making mistakes. Or there may be a retreat from engagement in the supervision process on some level, whether a change in attitude or in job performance. A pattern of tardiness or missed supervision sessions is a red flag. And more than likely, there were several flapping yellow flags missed before the relationship reached this point.

The work we do is difficult. We expect a great deal from our trainees as they become more independent clinical practitioners. The learning and application are constant.

A balanced approach to supervisory support is critical. Supervisors should have high expectations, but also remember how difficult the provider's path can be. If a supervisor can recall how hard the training process was for themselves, it opens the door to empathy and compassion. The supervisor should help re-establish contact between the trainee and their goals, to remind them of what they hope to accomplish. The supervisor should strive to foster the belief that the process is infinitely worth it. As training unfolds, the trainee may feel evaluated and become defensive. Balanced supervision does not aim to harm self-esteem, but instead to build confidence and comfort in the acquired skill set.

In those moments where the trainee may feel defeated, the supervisor must be supportive and empathetic. Help the trainee find humor in the telling of difficulties; help the trainee remember that no matter how tough the circumstances, it is not the end of the world. If it helps the trainee, the supervisor can remind them of the emerging assessment skills they can begin to rely on, the problem-solving and critical thinking skills they can use to identify next steps or extricate themselves from sticky situations. Above all, the supervisor must assess this change in the trainee's behavior. Doing so creates the opportunity to provide support where it is needed most.

FEAR OF MAKING MISTAKES

For fledgling trainees, making mistakes can be upsetting and sometimes even humiliating. Errors during ABA intervention sessions might call attention to lack of preparation and, sometimes, lack of skill. They can be embarrassing and impact a trainee's self esteem as they proceed through the training program. Making mistakes during intervention may lead to more intense behavior from the client: more aggression, reduced cooperation or higher rate of stereotypy. Blunders can erode confidence, both in the trainee and the client.

It is essential to not let shame get in the way of progress. Either the trainee is incorrectly assessing the impact of mistakes, or the supervisor is allowing too many mistakes to happen, to the detriment of the trainee's capacity to learn. Both are fixable. Distress over mistakes can become the impetus to positively alter the trajectory of training. If the supervisor has miscalculated, it's a great opportunity to model how to respond to a mistake. Herein lies the value of setting the right expectations for what happens in supervision. You will be able to graciously acknowledge that you miscalculated, and that you will adjust the level of support accordingly without harming your credibility or making the trainee feel they let you (or themself) down.

The other possibility is that the trainee's fear of making mistakes is due to them incorrectly interpreting what constitutes a mistake and inaccurately assessing the aftermath of a mistake. If so, the supervisor needs to help them more accurately assess the complete context. For example, if the client is exhibiting increased oppositional behavior, the trainee may tend to presume it is their fault, that it must be due to some mistake they have made. But another explanation could be that the trainee has hit upon a fundamental challenge for the client and is actually on the right path. Perhaps the only mistake was not anticipating the client's response! Or they may have uncovered a skill deficit that is impeding the client's progress. That is valuable information. The only mistake would be not to do something about it. The client response to events during ABA intervention sessions are clues to areas of behavioral concern and areas of skill deficit. It is a good thing for the client and trainee to have these moments, because it can move intervention in a more productive direction.

Sometimes these moments occur as a trainee conducts probes: the instruction format goes beyond what has been done previously. The trainee tries something new, or changes what is expected, to see how the student responds. While probes should be systematic, thoughtful and guided by clinical judgment, if something goes wrong or the client fails, it provides important information and allows us to identify that either the client is not ready or there is some adjustment that needs to be made. The only mistake would have been to not conduct the probe. Without the probe you might have spent more time than necessary at the current level, thereby slowing down progress.

Mistakes are learning opportunities. During debrief, the trainee should describe what they could have done differently, and how alternative decisions might have affected the outcome. Even if the outcome was optimal, they can still benefit from describing the rationales for the decisions they made during the instruction session, e.g., how quickly they faded prompts, when they introduced a new target, or the level of reinforcement they provided.

When Thomas Edison described the process of inventing the lightbulb, he said:

"I didn't fail. I found more than ten thousand ways that won't work. Every wrong attempt discarded was another step forward."

BF Skinner similarly commented:

"A failure is not always a mistake, it may simply be the best one can do under the circumstances. The real mistake is to stop trying."

Rescue Me! Even when the trainee is receptive and buy-in for the process is present, there will be times they will hope to be "saved." ABA intervention is complex and challenging. John McEachin once said, in a way only he can deliver; "Well, it's not rocket science. It's harder." There are times in an ABA intervention session when everyone is safe, but the session has taken a wrong turn and the trainee has that "deer in the headlights" expression. It can be tough to be a part of. If this is the beginning of the supervisory process and the trainee is clearly in over their head and has no knowledge of what to do, then an intervention from the supervisor may be called for, at the lowest level necessary to get the session moving in a better direction.

However, for trainees further along in the process, a session can go a bit pear-shaped due to something the trainee missed, but they can recover from it if they just remember their training and work through it. In these instances, the supervisor must resist the temptation to rescue the trainee, and not be too quick to make the problem the trainee was struggling with disappear. Rescuing them would be counterproductive. The supervisor may be trying to help, but needs to keep in mind the objective: the trainee relying on themself and their burgeoning skill set. Otherwise, the supervisor slows progress towards greater confidence and independence.

The supervisory relationship may suffer damage, too. The trainee may feel resentment, whether for the supervisor "showing them up," not ending the misery sooner, or making the trainee feel less able to do the job. Ultimately, if the trainee believes in the process, they know they have to work through adversity and not expect rescuing. If the supervisor is too quick to rescue the trainee, it undermines trust in their ability.

When the trainee has one of those amazing sessions where everything goes well and the client responds exactly as intended, it's a beautiful thing. The trainee was focused, yet comfortable. Each trial built on the previous one. The timing was spot on, and progression could be seen as the session unfolded. The supervisor may truly be hard pressed to find fault. Following such sessions, the debrief should focus on how intentionally the trainee operated, how aware they were of the "rightness" of their decisions. But a supervisor will know that they have hit the training bullseye when the trainee embraces both the successes of a carefully run session and the failures forcing reflection and introspection. The trainee should hope that challenging situations arise, since that provides a greater learning opportunity. And the reality is that in more typical sessions things are less than perfect, providing a greater opportunity to evaluate how well the trainee is making adjustments.

AVOIDANCE OF PROVIDING CORRECTIVE FEEDBACK

Just as being offended by corrective feedback—taking it personally or as unfair criticism—can be a supervision blocker, so can the supervisor's inability or unwillingness to provide that correction in the first place. Let's consider why this may occur and some possible solutions.

Providing corrective feedback is an underappreciated skill that requires active development. A supervisor hesitant to give corrective feedback should take stock. What are the variables preventing this from happening? Perhaps the supervisor is worried about alienating the trainee or provoking defensiveness. Maybe the supervisor believes corrective feedback will be received as judgmental, evaluative, personal or simply mean. Being careful to set the right expectations goes a long way toward mitigating such reactions. The supervisor should develop rationales that resonate with the trainee and use graduated exposure to the extent necessary.

If the issue lies more within the supervisor, they can seek guidance from a mentor or colleague. Practicing this skill to overcome confidence issues will help. Perhaps convening a peer group specific to addressing further development of supervisory skills is an option. A compassionate supervisor must be able to provide feedback in the right dosage, at the right moment, with the right content delivered, in the right tone. Working through this issue will increase the supervisor's ability to provide training more ably.

COMPASSION AND CONTROVERSY

One aspect of being a compassionate and clinically sensitive practitioner seems oxymoronic at first blush: possessing assuredness and not shying away from controversy. This is especially relevant if something must be addressed or debunked to maintain the integrity and availability of ABA methodology. Supervision can be a controversial topic, as illustrated in the following examples.

BALANCING CURRICULUM UPDATES (CLIENT-FOCUS) VS. ADVANCING INTERVENTION SKILLS (STAFF-FOCUS)

Supervision means different things to different people. For some, especially third-party players, it means updating curriculum content and modifying treatment protocols. This mentality derives from a model where the interventionist is merely a technician, only capable of carrying out fully scripted protocols that are developed by the clinical expert. There is no expectation for the interventionist to analyze the full constellation of variables that are impacting the client and how the client is responding. They are not expected to make strategy adjustments on the spot, nor are they meant to innovate in the selection of curriculum. In fact, they are generally forbidden from deviating from a carefully scripted protocol because they are not qualified to make such decisions, nor do they have sufficient training to be able to do so.

During session overlaps, there is a dissonance for the supervisor to address. Should the focus be on the client or the trainee? On the one hand, programmatic changes are clearly important, and curriculum needs to be continually updated. This clearly benefits the client and is part of the role of the supervisor. In this chapter, though, we have chosen to emphasize the other part of the supervisor's role because it is the one most neglected. And by neglecting the professional development of interventionists we are actually neglecting the most important way to maximize the progress of clients.

In our method of progressive ABA supervision, our goal is to develop a fully proficient interventionist with both clinical skills and a knowledge of individualized curriculum, which will benefit the client more over the long-term. Unlike many agencies where the interventionist is referred to as a behavior technician, we call them treatment analysts. The aspiring treatment analyst will be able to make curricular adjustments in the timeliest manner and will be providing the most productive intervention during the times when the supervisor is not there, which of course is the majority of intervention time.

In other models of ABA supervision, the client and curriculum adjustments are the overwhelming priorities, and this can be a disadvantage in the long run. In day-to-day practice there is often drift toward curriculum and programmatic updates. Training becomes more about programming than developing the trainee's intervention skills. It is seductive to be able to produce immediate change in the client's performance, and less immediately gratifying to achieve that through staff development.

Another reason why the preponderance of feedback during supervisory sessions is primarily focused on programming may be that this is safer territory for both the supervisor and the trainee, a less controversial area to focus on. Feedback mainly involves tweaks to current program phases, adapting curriculum to address targets more specifically, or adjusting the wording in instruction trials. These adjustments are concrete, easily accessible and typically result in quick, positive changes. This feedback is less apt to be taken evaluatively by those receiving it. A focus on the curriculum—and by extension, how the client responds to the adjustments—may be received as less personal, less judgmental.

A supervisory focus on assessment and critical thinking reinforces the notion that staff training is the priority. Of course, our ABA treatment goals include measurable and meaningful progress for the children we work with. But that can best be attained and then maintained if we embrace the following notion: supervision focused on increasing a trainee's proficiency in assessment and critical thinking will lead to the best outcomes. When looking back to the start of successful ABA intervention, the growth and expansion resulted more from staff expertise than tweaks to curriculum and programming.

Supervisors want their trainees to be successful. Further, they want the clients receiving ABA intervention to grow. The team wants the parents to see the ABA intervention working, the interplay between the trainee, supervisor and child resulting in positive change. The pressure to provide this connection to hope and progress can be overwhelming at times. So, feedback concerned with curriculum becomes a big draw. The supervisor tweaks the program, the trainee immediately puts it into effect, and everyone is gratified when what was recommended works. It's tempting to celebrate, no doubt.

But upon more critical examination, this success is often grounded in the short-term, and often addresses programmatic "symptoms" rather than the core issues that need to be comprehensively addressed. There is deeper satisfaction and joy associated with the trainee discovering those tweaks and adjustments for themself. Even if it takes a little longer, the benefit is more enduring. And the change in the child resulting from more independent application of intervention skill results in ABA treatment being reciprocal. It becomes what it should always be: an active exchange for both the interventionist and the child.

SUPERVISION MINIMUMS

Another controversial topic is the number of monthly hours allocated for supervision. It is common practice in many clinical settings providing ABA-based treatment to individuals with autism that supervisors spend a set amount of time with clients and staff across the month. Typically, the supervision sessions are few and far between, a minimum that fulfills basic business requirements and allows for more clients per supervisor, but impacts the ABA treatment delivery and ultimately, the client's outcome. This bare minimum is not enough to accomplish a progressive supervisory mission. Direct-line staff require sufficient supervisory time to help them develop a higher level of autonomy during those between times, when the supervisor is not present, so they'll be able to help the client more effectively in the long run.

FINAL THOUGHTS

The primary role of a supervisor is to mentor, to help trainees hone their skill set to become ever more effective in ABA intervention. The mission is about helping trainees achieve their greatest potential. It is inspiring them so they can attain higher expectations both of themselves and of the ABA intervention they provide to their clients. Excellent supervision is about high expectations and profound humility; it is all about the trainee. The supervisor should aim for the trainee to be better than the supervisor was.

So, the supervision sessions have been defined and the objectives discussed. The format has been established and the inoculations continue. The trainee understands the rationales behind the process and is invested in its progression with the supervisor. The interactive style has been individualized and refined. The discussions are lively and collaborative. The trainee is beginning to beat the supervisor on providing feedback, describing on their own what should be different, how that would unfold, and why. Supervision becomes a familiar and comfortable process, consistent in its approach to addressing targets patiently and thoroughly. The big picture comes into focus as a horizon to aim for and achieve. It is prudent to remember this is a living process, evolutionary, and adjustments are ongoing.

With all this in mind, the considerations below attempt to encapsulate the incredibly complex environment supervision occupies.

- **The first concern is that the trainee loves and looks forward to supervision**
  Begin the supervisory relationship with an initial talk. Include a definition of the mission, define the roles for trainer and trainee, develop trainee goals, inoculate, challenge, build trust and motivation.

- **Develop an individualized supervision framework for each trainee**
  This is a structure for ongoing skill development with flexibility built in as the process unfolds and as each trainee brings their own unique needs to the training sessions.

- **Teach the framework of how supervision will be provided as the relationship unfolds**
  Supervision relies on effective ABA teaching techniques. The supervisor must have a firm understanding of those techniques and how to individualize them to each trainee.

- **Schedule and format supervisory sessions**
  Aim to systematically build skill progression in every session. The focus is on the trainee's growth. By improving the trainee's clinical skills, their clients will reap the benefit.

- **Remember short- and long-term goal connectivity**
  Review progress and debrief after difficulties. Maintain motivation. Celebrate mistakes and reframe them as learning opportunities. Model for the trainee the fact that we never stop learning.

- **Be patient**
  Don't rush the process. Keep the objectives in focus. Pick your times to debrief.

- **Be unobtrusive during treatment sessions**
  Observe quietly, keeping track of information as it unfolds that will ultimately inform the supervision debrief. Be present, but not distracting.

- **Supervision is a parallel process**
  The same behavioral instruction guidelines that the trainee should be following apply to supervision: make yourself a conditioned reinforcer; break skills down; be proactive; provide the least assistive prompt that can get the job done; shape; provide positive and corrective feedback; teach toward generalization. And make it as enjoyable and natural as possible!

- **Use relatable, relevant examples**
  This helps clarify information for the trainee and increases the likelihood that it will stick with them.

- **When suggestions or corrections are made, provide rationales**
  Don't just tell the trainee what to do differently. Tell them why. The trainee will better grasp the concepts and more likely apply them more generally.

- **Corrective feedback is necessary**
  Get comfortable with using it. But be sure to monitor how correction is received.

- **Allow for critical feedback yourself!**
  Involve the trainee in the discussion. Pick times for the trainee to share their thoughts on the process. Elicit critical feedback and model reception of this information.

- **Don't settle**
  Continually strive for improvement. The trainees should be adding to their knowledge base, not resting on it. There is always opportunity to learn.

- **Don't get married to a strict session agenda**
  Have a framework. But be flexible. If possible, use what was observed as the material to discuss and promote further skill development.

- **Always be on the lookout for supervision blockers**

THE TAKEAWAY

Supervision is not a "black" *vs.* "white" proposition. There is a range of effective strategies to be used, depending on the trainee and where they are in the process. You are always balancing benefits and tradeoffs when choosing a path. These are important to always factor into your exercise of clinical judgment and decision-making:

- In-the-moment vs. delayed feedback

- Prescriptive vs. psychoeducational delivery

- Intervention technique vs. curriculum modification

- Corrective feedback and reinforcement

- Prompt in advance vs. allow error to happen

- Long- vs. short-term goals

- Trainee vs. client focus

References

Ala'i-Rosales, S., & Zeug, N. (2010). Three important things to consider when starting intervention for a child diagnosed with autism. *Behavior Analysis in Practice*, 3(2), 54-55.

Ben-Itzchak, E., & Zachor, D. A. (2007). The effects of intellectual functioning and autism severity on outcome of early behavioral intervention for children with autism. *Research in Developmental Disabilities*, 28, 287-303.

Dixon, D. R., Linstead, E., Granpeesheh, D., Novack, M. N., French, R., Stevens, E., Stevens, L., & Powell, A. (2016). An evaluation of the impact of supervision intensity, supervisor qualifications, and caseload on outcomes in the treatment of autism spectrum disorder. *Behavior Analysis in Practice*, 9, 339-348.

Eldevik, S., Hastings, R. P., Hughes, J. C., Jahr, E., Eikeseth, S., & Cross, S. (2009). Meta-analysis of early intensive behavioral intervention for children with autism. *Journal of Clinical Child and Adolescent Psychology*, 38(3), 439-450.

Fenske, E. C., Zalenski, S., Krantz, P. J., & McClannahan, L. E. (1985). Age at intervention and treatment outcome for autistic children in a comprehensive intervention program. *Analysis and Intervention for Developmental Disabilities*, 5, 49-58.

Harris, S. L., & Handleman, J. S. (2000). Age and IQ at intake as predictors of placement for young children with autism: a four-to six-year follow-up. *Journal of Autism and Developmental Disorders*, 30, 137-142.

Leaf, J. B., Leaf, J. A., Milne, C., Taubman, M., Oppenheim-Leaf, M., Torress, N., Townley-Cochran, D., Leaf, R., McEachin, J., & Yoder, P. (2017). An evaluation of a behaviorally based social skills group for individuals diagnosed with autism spectrum disorder. *Journal of Autism and Developmental Disorders*, 47, 243-259.

Leaf, J. B., Leaf, R., McEachin, J., Taubman, M., Ala'i-Rosales, S., Ross, R. K., Smith, T, & Weiss, M. J. (2016). Applied Behavior Analysis is a Science and, Therefore, Progressive. *Journal of Autism and Developmental Disorders*, 46, 720-731.

Leaf, J. B., Taubman, M., Bloomfield, S., Palos-Rafuse, L. I., McEachin, J. J., Leaf, R. B., et al. (2009). Increasing social skills and prosocial behavior for three children diagnosed with autism through the use of a teaching package. *Research in Autism Spectrum Disorder*, 3, 275–289.

Leaf, R. B., Taubman, M., McEachin, J. J., Leaf, J. B., & Tsuji, K. H. (2011). A program description of a community-based intensive behavioral intervention program for individuals with autism spectrum disorders. *Education and Treatment of Children*, 34, 259-285.

Lovaas, O. I. (1987). Behavioral treatment and normal education and intellectual functioning in young autistic children. *Journal of Consulting and Clinical Psychology*, 55, 3-9.

Phillips, E. L., Phillips, E. A., Fixsen, D. L., & Wolf, M. M. (1971). Achievement place: Modification of the behaviors of predelinquent boys within a token economy. *Journal of Applied Behavior Analysis*, 4, 45–59.

Phillips, E. L., Phillips, E. A., Fixsen, D. L., & Wolf, M. M. (1974). *The teaching-family handbook (2nd ed.)*. Lawrence, KS: University Press of Kansas.

Stokes, T. F., & Baer, D. B. (1977). An implicit technology of generalization. *Journal of Applied Behavior Analysis*, 10, 349-367.

CHAPTER 8

SUPPORTING PARENTS

For an ABA supervisor there is a strong parallel between parent support and effective staff training. In both, the main objective is developing competency and promoting the greatest independence possible. It will be necessary for the parent to understand the basic principles of behavior, how to identify the functions of behavior and how to promote replacement behavior. As described in Chapter 7, we recommend using a psychoeducational approach that will give parents the tools to figure things out on their own and decrease reliance on someone else to tell them how to solve their parenting challenges.

UNDERSTANDING THE CHALLENGE PARENTS FACE

Catherine Maurice shared her experience in *Let Me Hear Your Voice* (1994). It is a gut-wrenching read and describes how exponentially harder it is being the parent of one child diagnosed with autism—let alone two! She described the range of emotions that tug at you when you first suspect your child might have autism, and the desperate search for any evidence to assure yourself that everything is okay. Some parents discuss their fears with their partner and the response might be, "Don't worry, everything is okay," perhaps as much an attempt to quell their own misgivings as much as their partner's. There is self-doubt. "Am I overreacting? Do I dare say it aloud to my friends and family?" When they can no longer bear the uncertainty, they may seek out a pediatrician or other trusted professional. They might hear what they dared not hope, that all kids are different, their child will surely have a growth spurt, and everything will be fine. But it may not be the correct advice.

As the developmental gap continues to widen and parents continually confront how different their child is from their peers, then begins the next chapter of the nightmare: getting a diagnostic evaluation. Just finding a diagnostician can be a challenge. Should they seek the advice of a psychologist? Psychiatrist? Neurologist, occupational therapist, speech pathologist? Maybe all of them? How can they know who is really an expert? If they are "lucky" they will get a definitive diagnosis. And even if they already suspect their child has autism, it is still gut-wrenching to get confirmation. Parents have shared that it is similar to when a person who strongly suspects they have cancer and thinks they are fully prepared for the worst, but hearing a doctor say the words out loud is shattering.

Parents are then faced with the burden of planning a course of action and trying to assimilate overwhelming, often contradictory information. While trying to maintain rational decision-making there is a flood of emotion that may include anger—anger at the professionals who let them down, anger at their family for not being more supportive, anger at themselves for not following their gut. They lost precious time and are determined to make up for it. When they arrive at our doorstep, they may not know what questions to ask and probably don't know what they want. They may not be able to process all the information we want to share with them and could be skeptical about our advice.

Unlike therapeutic staff, parents face the additional challenge of being far more emotionally invested in the outcome. So, being objective can be extremely difficult. It pains them to see their child suffering and their first instinct is to prevent distress as much as possible. When that fails, parents do whatever it takes to placate their child. Allowing natural consequences to occur can be excruciating for parents! They just want their child to be happy, and they don't see how that ends up depriving the child of opportunities to develop tolerance of adversity. It feels antithetical to being a loving parent.

SETTING THE STAGE FOR SUCCESS

For parents of a child diagnosed with autism, the initial talk between the parent and the interventionist should build meaningful rationales and reinforcement for participating in the process, and inoculation for how challenging the work will be. This will include an introduction to the behavior analytic framework for understanding and changing behavior. It needs to be clear that instead of telling parents what they should do, you will help them learn the necessary principles enabling them to develop effective strategies to support their child. It will be essential that they fully understand and embrace the model.

For many reasons, it is completely understandable that this does not fulfill the parents' original expectations. When they first come to you, they are probably overwhelmed and possibly even in crisis. Even as their child begins receiving behavioral intervention, there is still no immediate respite for them at home. For all mothers and fathers, it is difficult enough being the best parent you can be. Now compound that with all the additional challenges that autism can bring, and you can understand how they want the quickest fix possible. They just want to know what they should do when their child won't go to sleep and instead wanders the house during the night. Or how to address their child's extremely limited diet and its impact on family meals. Or what to do when a trip to the local market turns into a loud and embarrassing tantrum. And, for sure, they want to get their child toilet trained.

When we seek the guidance of a professional, be it a physician, an auto mechanic or a plumber, the expectation is for them to solve whatever the issue may be. The clinically sensitive ABA supervisor should anticipate and understand the parents' reluctance to take on responsibility for figuring out strategies, and having to be patient with slowly accumulating the additional expertise that is necessary to effectively parent a child with special needs.

Many ABA supervisors do not have children, let alone a child on the spectrum. Therefore, it is impossible to fully understand a parent's perspective. Until you have had a child you simply don't understand the incredibly deep love a parent feels for their child. Anything a parent does that causes sadness goes directly against their protective instinct, even when they know their job as a parent is not always making your child happy.

The job of the ABA supervisor is to support the parent empathically, but with clarity about the most effective way to produce behavior change. It begins with describing the psychoeducational service model they will be participating in. With their collaboration, identify the goals for behavior change in the child and describe the process that will allow them to become effective behavior change agents. Break the model down into achievable components. Carve out steps that are small enough that the parents could see themselves successfully carrying out a behavior intervention plan. Help them see the way the component parts build a comprehensive whole, a skill set that will enable them to analyze problem behavior and promote appropriate alternative behavior. With your guidance, the parents will be shareholders in their child's ABA intervention program.

It is essential to ensure that parents don't feel guilty that they need your assistance. We validate that their approach to parenting would work with most children, but their child is not like most, and at times reacts quite differently than neurotypical children. That's part of autism. So, we will teach them how to deal with the unique challenges they face as a parent. We don't want them to feel in the slightest that they are incompetent parents. It's the reason we prefer the term "parent support" rather than the more common term, "parent training." Who would want to feel that they need to be "trained" to be a parent? They simply need support.

In addition to describing the model, it's critical to prepare them for the emotional roller coaster they will experience in attempting to get comfortable with a different way of responding to their child and often seeing that it doesn't work right away. They will likely experience tremendous discouragement when the child's behavior intensifies in response to their new strategy. Help them reframe their experience to recognize that sometimes an escalation is a sign that a plan is working. When we change the way we respond to behavior, often that behavior intensifies because what worked for the child before is not working now. This is not the time to abandon ship, but rather stay the course. A key to successful parent support is helping them develop the coping skills necessary to stay the course in the face of emotionally distressing behavior.

Parents being raw, and in pain, is not easy to witness, let alone to intentionally allow. But just as the parents need to allow their child the space to encounter adversity and learn how to cope with delay and exercise their tolerance muscle, we should not shy away from exposing parents to situations just because we fear it will make them uncomfortable. Facilitating contact with uncomfortable situations with a goal of discovery should be seen as the highest degree of compassion.

UNDERSTANDING FUNCTION

When we have completed the preparation stage, the next step will be building the foundation of knowledge in behavior principles that will guide them in anticipating and responding to their child's behavior. The foundation for a sturdy framework to parenting is the understanding that all behavior occurs for a reason; even the most seemingly counterproductive behavior is under the influence of variables that we can identify, if we know what to look for. So, the first step is helping parents understand that behaviors make sense. In ABA's nomenclature, there are understandable functions for all behaviors. They occur for a reason and by understanding the reason, we can effectively change behaviors and find appropriate replacements serving the same general purpose.

In helping parents understand the connection between behavior, antecedent events, and consequences, we recommend that the discussion not start with their own child. Beginning the process with examples of behavior demonstrated by other children, in videos or vignettes, increases objectivity and reduces the emotions associated with their own child. It provides a safe place to practice and develop confidence. Once they have a basic understanding of assessing functions as applied to behavior in general, they will be better able to understand and engage with their own child.

For illustrative purposes, use everyday examples parents find informative, interesting, and most importantly, applicable to their own situation. Why does someone smoke cigarettes even though it is expensive, will cause health issues, results in early death and affects the health of their loved ones? Why does someone become a bully? Why are people negative? Why do people perseverate on topics? What is the purpose of that self-stimulatory behavior? Why doesn't that person join conversations with others? When people gain an understanding of what makes others tick, it prepares them better to make a constructive response to behavior.

It is important that parents understand that there are many potential reasons (functions) for behaviors, and that those reasons can be ever-changing. The reason someone smokes as a teenager is different from when they are an adult. One child's self-stimulatory behavior occurs for very different reasons than another's.

Eventually, you move to behaviors that are more personal and impactful in the parents' lives. There is no timetable defining how long it will take for a parent to be able to skillfully perform "functional analysis." But once they have a full understanding, it's time to help them identify replacement behaviors based upon the function, making it clear that there are likely multiple possible replacement behaviors. Start with general examples and systematically move toward identifying their own child's potential replacement behaviors. The following table illustrates some typical examples of alternative behavior to teach based on the hypothesized function(s) of problem behavior.

Hypothesized Function(s)	Possible Replacement Behaviors
Avoidance or Escape (unpreferred activity or request)	▪ Communicate desire to avoid through speech ("no," "not now," "uh-uh") or through gestures (e.g., shaking head, hand movement) or pictures (e.g., stop sign, no, etc.) ▪ Identify why child may want to avoid tasks and make them more preferable (e.g., break task down, make it fun, help child become competent) ▪ Teach skills to increase engagement and attention ▪ Teach coping skills to reduce frustration or anxiety ▪ Teach negotiation ▪ Teach to be a good listener
Attention Seeking	▪ Teach pro-social behaviors that would result in receiving attention ▪ Teach skills that would likely result in recognition
Stereotypic Behaviors (Self-Stimulation)	▪ Teach skills that provide a means to receive stimulation (e.g., leisure, play and social skills)
Requests/Access	▪ Teach a communication skill so that desire can be communicated (e.g., speech, gestures, pictures) ▪ It may also be important to teach child to tolerate not getting what they want or to patiently tolerate waiting
Control	▪ Give child areas of control (e.g., what clothes to wear, where to sit, etc.) ▪ Teach to be a good listener ▪ Teach child to make choices ▪ Teach flexibility ▪ Teach coping skills so they can tolerate when they don't have control ▪ Teach negotiation and compromise
Relieve Frustration, Stress & Anxiety	▪ Employ graduated exposure or systematic desensitization prior to teaching coping skills ▪ Teach coping skills (e.g., deep breathing, muscle relaxation, self-talk, guided imagery)

BECOMING A REINFORCEMENT DISPENSER

Once there is an understanding of appropriate and individualized replacement behaviors, the content of your support moves to how to use reinforcement to increase those desired behaviors. The parents need to become effective reinforcement dispensers. This means first identifying the things they can use that will be effective as reinforcement. From their functional assessment exercises, parents will already have identified some very important reinforcers, such as attention. You can brainstorm with them items and activities that their child shows interest in, and the access can be controlled by the parent. The second step is getting good at the timing. Often it is as simple as "catching the child being good." This is an observational skill that requires practice. When you can observe jointly, give the parent a quota and a time limit. Challenge them to find moments of reinforcement-worthy behavior. In order to meet their quota, they may have to be flexible with the standard they adopt for earning reinforcement. If their expectation is unrealistically high, they will miss important opportunities to reinforce improvement. You will be shaping their ability to shape their child's behavior.

OBSTACLES

We often hear, "we have tried it, but it just didn't work." It will be necessary to gently point out that if it didn't work, it wasn't actually reinforcement. Reinforcement is defined by its effect on behavior or performance. If the parents give contingent access to something they think the child likes and it doesn't result in increasing the desired behavior, then it wasn't a reinforcer. Either the reinforcer was too weak, the effort required to perform the behavior was too much, or it wasn't implemented consistently at a sufficiently high level.

Finding, developing and using reinforcement is not easy and it does not come naturally to most of us. But everyone will get better at using reinforcement with practice—lots of practice. The challenge is that it requires a lot of work and there may not be sufficient payoff in the form of improved behavior, which then leads to burn-out. Another issue for parents is what the child says they like may not actually correspond to what is truly motivating. Or the parent overgeneralizes from what they find reinforcing or what is presumed to be reinforcing to children in general, but it turns out is not reinforcing to their child. Parents knowing what is reinforcing for them is great, but that does not mean the reinforcement they love is motivating to someone else. The bottom line is, without the correct reinforcement, our methodology does not work.

Another potential obstacle is that the child may have an extremely limited repertoire of reinforcers due to a narrow range of interests. Or it may be that many of the reinforcers that are motivating to them are completely under the child's control, meaning they can access it without having to fulfill any behavioral requirement. This will require building new reinforcers so that the child will be motivated by a broader range of commonly available activities and items whose availability can be regulated. Having a wide variety of reinforcers keeps motivation high and reduces the likelihood of satiation. There's nothing worse than a parent's "golden go-to" losing its power! There will also be the added benefit of broadening the child's range of interests, resulting in a richer, more fulfilling life.

THE FINER POINTS OF REINFORCEMENT

Contingency is another essential concept. Being contingent means if a behavior occurs, reinforcement will consistently be provided. It also means the reinforcer is *never* provided if it wasn't earned. And it means parents have to be 100% comfortable withholding an unearned reinforcer. Being contingent means meltdowns will happen. Parents will need to be able to ride out a tantrum.

If parents are making watching TV or using an iPad contingent, they need to anticipate withholding these reinforcers when they have not been earned. This may require figuring out how to keep the child constructively occupied when they don't have their most preferred activity available. Parents need to consider if this is a challenge they can see themselves successfully accomplishing. They will have to weigh short-term pain against long-term gain. This means choosing carefully the behavior they want to tackle, the skill they want to replace it with, and a reinforcer they can be contingent with.

Additional reinforcement topics that need to be covered are schedules, using graduated reinforcement, thinning, and transitioning reinforcers. We are not expecting an expert-level depth of knowledge, but simple and practical concepts like beginning with frequent reinforcement and systematically moving to an intermittent schedule. Parents will also need to plan an eventual transition from artificial reinforcers to intrinsic (e.g., pride in one's accomplishments), and weaning from tangible to symbolic and social reinforcers (e.g., praise).

CORRECTIVE FEEDBACK

Praise and other reinforcement are a clear signal that lets the child know they are on the right track. But what about those moments when they veer off track? That's the time for honest feedback from the parents. The child needs a clear and consistent signal that they have crossed the line, e.g., "That's too loud," or "That's not safe." Over time, corrective feedback becomes meaningful because it is paired with nonreinforcement. Feedback should be clear, succinct and resolute. Parents should avoid lengthy discussion, debate or negotiation; that could be reinforcing the problem behavior by giving it more attention than it deserves. The feedback should be straightforward and objective. For example, a statement like, "That hurt my feelings," is not the best choice because it defines appropriate vs. inappropriate according to how tolerant the other person is. If the person is generous and does not take offense at the behavior, it should not let the child off the hook. Rude is rude; there should be a consistent standard that is established, with feedback that defines problem behavior according to that standard rather than how another person feels. Discussion about the impact of a child's behavior should be reserved for proactive teaching, done at a time when the child is receptive and provides a rationale for why it's important to be polite. But saying, "That hurt my feelings," as feedback when the child is not receptive could actually be reinforcing, if the timing is not right.

Similarly, a threat is not really feedback. A threat is actually a failure to implement a consequence when problem behavior has already occurred. In the early stages of teaching, parents can give reminders such as, "Remember the rules when you're playing with the dog," but only in advance, and with the goal of fading such prompts as the child is more consistently successful. Once they have broken the rule, there should be feedback followed immediately by consequence. Second, third and fourth chances only teach the child that they don't really have to follow the rule. Most importantly, we have to help parents understand that corrective feedback is an essential tool for everyone's learning. We learn just as much—if not more!—from correction than we do from reinforcement.

PUTTING IT ALL TOGETHER

The next focus will be on methods for teaching new skills. This means becoming familiar with shaping, prompting, prompt fading, chaining, and task analysis. Once again, parents don't need to know it in a professional manner, just practically. Provide lots of everyday examples such as how we learn an athletic skill, how we learn to choose clothing and dress independently, how to play the piano, cooking macaroni and cheese, washing our hands. All these skills can be taught using behavioral teaching methods.

Becoming proactive in teaching is essential. Otherwise, people tend to default to reactive strategies. What we do proactively is the most important part of behavior change, and the part that tends to be overlooked. Proactive teaching means not waiting until a problem happens. Our goal is to prevent problem behavior by teaching the child skills that will make acting out unnecessary. Teaching needs to be done under ideal conditions, when both parents and child are available, attentive and receptive. Work with parents to make a plan for when and where this will occur, so they don't have to compete for the child's attention: not during or right after a meltdown, but rather when everyone is in a good mood.

Of course, reactive procedures are necessary because there will always be occasions of problem behavior, despite our best efforts. Parents need to be emotionally prepared to work through a meltdown in the most constructive manner possible, which many times means simply not letting the behavior pay off, i.e., don't give in, don't provide attention, and don't allow escape from necessary duties. They should allow natural consequences to occur, e.g., "We can discuss this when you are calm." Reactive procedures can get parents through a crisis and potentially teach the child what *not* to do, but the main focus should be on proactive teaching, which is aimed at teaching the child what *to do*.

Finally, it's time to put the concepts together. Identify a simple behavior problem that the parents have not previously tackled and help them come up with a plan. Make it their plan, even if you have had to shape it. The more they see it as their plan, the more they will own it and follow it. Suggest that they pilot the plan under ideal conditions. Discuss it, plan it, role-play it. Guide them to identify possible pitfalls—how might the plan go awry, and then how to prevent that outcome, or how to make adjustments if necessary.

THE TAKEAWAY

Giving parents the tools to help them become more effective with their children will be critical to their child's success. They have an enormous burden that far exceeds typical parenting, and they are not professionals (nor should they try to be). So, we need to provide them with a lot of support on this difficult journey. Some of what we ask them to do is counterintuitive, so they have to learn a different way of parenting. We need to use all the clinical tools we have to be active listeners, be relatable, be sensitive, empathic and full of compassion. Be patient, but do the work!

References

Maurice, C. (1994). *Let me hear your voice: A family's triumph over autism.* New York City, New York: Ballantine Books.

CHAPTER 9

FAMILY DYNAMICS

JAMISON DAYHARSH & RON LEAF

The vast majority of books and research articles about Autism Spectrum Disorder deal mainly with the individual with autism and how it affects their life (e.g., Lovaas, 1987; Lovaas et al., 1973; Sallows et al., 2005). With the exception of the work by Sandra Harris and her colleagues (e.g., Glasberg et al., 2006; Harris et al., 1983), very little is written about the family. However, careful attention must be given to treating the whole family, because the whole family is profoundly affected by autism, and the family will have a big impact on treatment outcome. Clearly, if it were not for the family, the child with autism would not have the best opportunities for improvement. There would not be the support and nurturing necessary to endure the challenges. It is ultimately the family that makes it happen.

Unless someone has had a child with autism, it is impossible to understand the pressures that mothers and fathers feel. It starts with the struggle to obtain a correct diagnosis and then moves on to sorting out hundreds of treatment options and having to deal with potentially condescending professionals with unsupportive attitudes and conflicting advice. It is natural that parents are not only devastated and depressed, but also infuriated with the process.

Historically, parents have also had to deal with tremendous guilt. Are they responsible for their child's disorder? Did they do something wrong during pregnancy? Did they make the wrong decision regarding the birthing method? Did they not spend enough time with their child? In the early days, professionals believed that parents were responsible for the child's disorder. It was observed that children interventionists saw in their clinics children who had autism had parents who were highly educated. This set the stage for parents being targeted as culprits. It was hypothesized that the parents must have been more interested in their career than their child and did not provide the care that the child needed. Eventually, it was shown that the high level of education of the parents was an artifact of better educated parents having the resources and knowledge to seek diagnosis and treatment.

Bruno Bettelheim (1967) asserted that mothers were responsible for their child's disorder. He labeled them as "refrigerator mothers." That is, they were cold and did not make an emotional connection with their child. Thus, their child withdrew from the world. Holding or Bonding Therapy is based upon this hypothesis. By holding their child for hours daily, they would form a bond and therefore facilitate their re-emergence into the world. When the emotional status of parents was examined more closely, it became clear that emotional distancing was a result of having a child with autism, not the cause. Not surprisingly, holding therapy was shown to be ineffective as a treatment (e.g., Mercer, 2013). But even today parents are still made to feel responsible for their child's disorder.

Tragically, there have been more recent therapies based upon the same old and disproven assumption of parent responsibility. These therapies are based upon the assumption that it is an emotional disorder based upon the absence of emotional bonding with parents (e.g., DIR/Floortime model; Wieder & Greenspan, 2003). In such therapy programs, play is used as a vehicle for establishing this presumably missing bond and the assumption is that once the emotional repair occurs, the child will emerge from the world of autism. It is Bettelheim repackaged!

Even though all these hypotheses of parents being at the root of their child's disorder have been refuted, some professionals today still treat parents with suspicion. Not only do they promote therapies designed to root out alleged parental psychopathology, but there also exist questions and speculation, by professionals who should know better than believing the parents did something to create the child's problem.

Besides having to deal with the anguish and perhaps guilt of having a child with a severe disability, parents bear the burden of finding the right treatment for their child. Typically, their life is consumed with therapies, driving to Speech and Occupational Therapy, having therapists tromp into their home all day long, getting an uncooperative child ready for school, attending team meetings, and visiting the psychologist for the dreaded reevaluation. In addition to this full-time job, they must become an expert in the treatment methodologies, not to mention learn enough about science to be able to protect themselves against quackery. It is no surprise that parents feel their child's entire existence and quality of life rests solely on their shoulders. What an absolutely incredible burden!

It is all too common for parents to become totally consumed and feel as though they have no choice other than sacrificing their own well-being and their family's well-being for the good of their child with autism. It is absolutely understandable that parents would do everything in their power to rescue their child with tremendous needs. Unfortunately, however, such a sacrifice is problematic in a number of ways that affect the parent, their partner, and their other children.

PARENTS CARING FOR THEMSELVES

All too often, parenting a child with autism becomes a profession. We do believe that parents must become knowledgeable enough to use specialized parenting methods and be able to effectively advocate for their child. However, a parent needs to maintain a balance between their child's needs and their own personal needs. We know that it sounds like psychobabble, but you must take care of yourself in order to be able to take care of others. If parents are unhappy and stressed, they simply cannot be as fresh as they need to be for the task at hand. It is impossible to be positive and energized if your entire life is consumed by your child.

Parents need to be able to find happiness in their lives in order to have the energy to care for their children. This is as true for children with autism as it is for typically developing children. Too often parents define happiness in terms of their child's progress, such as, "I cannot be happy as long as my child is suffering from autism." We understand this sentiment and perhaps we could compromise on striving for contentment in one's life, with contentment defined as not being miserable. Can you find room in your life for a special interest or hobby other than autism? If not, then you are trying to do too much and you are doomed to fail.

Denying your own needs will catch up with you sooner or later. Trying to be Superman or Superwoman is not a realistic goal. You are kidding yourself if you think you can be superhuman and you are being unfair to yourself if you think it is necessary to demonstrate superpowers to be a good parent. You can only do what is humanly possible. If you feel compelled to go to conferences, read about the latest "cures" for autism or scour the internet for new ideas, we recommend that you do it within limits. Spend time with your partner, with friends and most importantly take care of yourself! It is what your child needs. It is what your partner needs. It is what you need.

PARENTS CARING FOR THEIR PARTNERS

Any relationship, even the best, takes attention and ongoing work. As thrilled as parents are to have a new child in their family, it is a challenge. Besides a lack of sleep and a total change of routine and lifestyle, there are debates about expectations for the child, child-rearing practices, what time they should be in bed, where they should sleep... and the list never ends. Naturally, when a child with autism enters the family, there will be astronomically more stress upon the system. It is necessary to be proactive to ensure that the parenting team is coping with the additional stress.

One of the most essential things is to take care of the relationship. All too often children become the center of the relationship, thereby eroding its foundation. The relationship is also weakened when partners do not spend quality time together. Too often, the times that parents do manage to get away together are for things like a parent meeting, an IEP, or to discuss their child's progress. We highly recommend date nights on a regular basis. Weekly is not too often! It does not have to be extravagant. Maybe just a walk, a picnic or sitting on a park bench. We often hear parents say that their child will suffer if they are not there. We believe children may suffer a lot more if parents do not take a few hours for themselves.

What about when parents are concerned that there is no one to watch the children? Well, this may take creativity. Perhaps a family member or friend watch them, or parents can exchange baby-sitting services with other parents who have children with autism. Parents often fear that no one has the skills to watch their child properly. It is not necessary for the babysitter to be perfect, and it is certainly not realistic that they would be as completely attentive as the parents would be. The regression can be overcome, and in the long run, it is important for children to be able to tolerate less-than-perfect caregivers. The earlier parents can get their children, partners, and themselves into this wonderful habit, the better. The payoff will be that they can soon consider an occasional night away!

PARENTS CARING FOR THEIR OTHER CHILDREN

A family's neurotypical children are every bit as important as the child with autism. No parent intentionally pays more attention to one child over another. Parents often feel that later on, they will be able to more equally share their attention. Neurotypical children may express understanding and seeming acceptance that their sibling with autism needs a lot of attention. They probably have experienced that life is not so pleasant when their sibling with autism does not get enough attention and therefore go along with parents giving extra time to their sibling.

Even though neurotypical children may bravely express such a sentiment, it is a different issue emotionally. Although in their head they realize that their brother or sister requires a lot of attention, in their heart it is unavoidable to feel left out. This can lead to resentment. Then they feel guilty about their feelings, which only compounds the problem.

It is critical that they not only get their share of quality time and attention, but that they do not have to feel responsible for their brother or sister. They should not be expected to serve in the role of therapist or teacher. We understand it may be convenient for them to be a special playmate or be the model for teaching new skills, but it is generally not in their best interest. They need to fight and argue as well as wrestle and tickle and play chase and should not have to treat their sibling as special or needy. This is not only good for the neurotypical child, but also for their sibling with autism. The child with autism needs to learn to compete for attention and to be responsible for themselves, and the lesson starts at home with the family.

THE TAKEAWAY

It is completely understandable why parents of children with autism would focus their attention on treatment and the practical challenges that exist. But it will be essential for everyone's mental health that family happiness is front and center.

References

Glasberg, B. A., Martins, M., & Harris, S. L. (2006). Stress and coping among family members of individuals with autism. In M. G., Baron, J. Groden, G. Groden, & L. P. Lipsitt. *Stress and Coping in Autism* (pp. 277-301), Oxford University Press.

Harris, S. L., Wolchik, S. A., & Milch, R. E. (1983). Changing the speech of autistic children and their parents. *Child & Family Behavior Therapy*, 4(2-3), 151–173.

Lovaas, O. I. (1987). Behavioral treatment and normal educational and intellectual functioning in young autistic children. *Journal of Consulting and Clinical Psychology*, 55(1), 3–9.

Lovaas, O. I., Koegel, R., Simmons, J. Q., & Long, J. S. (1973). Some generalization and follow-up measures on autistic children in behavior therapy, 6(1), 131–165.

Mercer, J. (2013). Holding therapy: a harmful mental health intervention. *Focus on Alternative and Complementary Therapies*, 18, 70-76.

Sallows, G. O., & Graupner, T. D. (2005). Intensive behavioral treatment for children with autism: Four-year outcome and predictors. *American Journal on Mental Retardation*, 110, 417-438.

Wieder, S., & Greenspan, S. I. (2003). Climbing the symbolic ladder in the DIR model through Floortime/interactive play. *Autism*, 7(4), 425–435.

CHAPTER 10

REFLECTION

As we have shared throughout the book, being a compassionate and curious behaviorist is not a new concept. We think it is important to acknowledge that these ideas are deeply rooted in our history, but that the field drifted off course in more recent decades. We have been outspoken about how poor clinical implementation has adversely affected clients, families and the field. Although we are thrilled to reinfuse compassion into behaviorism, because it is *much, much* needed, we wonder why, given that these concepts have been around since the 1950s, is it only now regaining appreciation?

There are likely several factors. To start off, it seems that a great deal of our history is no longer taught. The newer generation of interventionists do appear to be familiar with the work of Mary Cover Jones, Joseph Wolpe or Sandra Harris, but the field has become so narrow that interventionists aren't familiar with clinical pioneers such as Carl Rogers, Albert Ellis or Hans Miller. Our hunch is that the largest factor leading to the rediscovery of our past is the rebound effect from how awful a lot of ABA services have become over the past couple of decades. There has been overreliance on standardized protocols, and interventionists are not being trained to be responsive to the myriad of variables affecting behavior moment by moment. They often do not consider their clients' opinions and demand their protocols be followed precisely, without question or discussion. Often the interventions are implemented poorly by unwitting interventionists who don't know any better. They are products of inadequate training. Add to that the dearth of effective supervision, and it makes sense there has been a severe backlash against ABA methodology, as well as a blanket shaming and blaming of the procedures promoted by our field (e.g., Devita-Raeburn, 2016; Ram, 2020). And no wonder there has been a movement to inject compassion and clinical sensitivity into behaviorism (e.g. Miller, 2021), when the reality is, if it had been done correctly, as the ABA pioneers intended it, those components would have been there all along.

Practitioners that don't form a therapeutic alliance, who are not active listeners and are not compassionate, also are not following guidance from the wealth of scholarly literature supporting these clinical skills in application and practice. They are not providing meaningful support leading to positive outcomes for our clientele. They are by definition not administering best-practice, ethical ABA; they are, therefore, not truly interventionists.

To be an effective interventionist requires extensive education and training in clinical skills, just like our pioneers knew more than a half a century ago. But in addition to looking at our past, examining other approaches, and understanding the literature, the methods and applications need to continue to improve, supported by rigorous empirical evaluation.

As we have discussed extensively in journal articles, e.g., *Applied Behavior Analysis is a Science and, Therefore, Progressive* (Leaf et al., 2016) and books e.g., *It Has to Be Said*, (Leaf et al., 2008) and *Clinical Judgment*, (Leaf et al., 2019) quality treatment must be highly individualized, and interventionists must be trained in and skillfully utilize clinical judgment. The needs of our clients are extremely diverse, but unfortunately, the vast majority of intervention is protocol-driven and rigid in its implementation. Conversely, there are behaviorists who fully recognize that every child is extremely different and that their behaviors can change second by second. Therefore, not all ABA is alike, just like not all politicians, physicians or chefs are alike.

There are interventionists who quickly resort to aversive methods of behavior change while others strive to be positive and engaging. There are interventionists who are impervious to the desires of their clients and their families. And there are interventionists who diligently listen and incorporate their client's perspectives. There are interventionists that don't have an ounce of clinical skill and there are interventionists that are sensitive and empathic. There are interventionists who are harsh and indifferent and there are interventionists who are compassionate.

When we worked with adults during deinstitutionalization in the early 1980s, we carefully listened to our clients' perspectives and wishes. We didn't always agree with their requests, but that did not mean in any way that we didn't hear and consider their perspective. But when a client with Prader-Willi Syndrome chose to consume three dinners per night while having a life-threatening eating disorder, we did everything to encourage them to eat more healthily. When we worked with clients who preferred violence as a means to obtain their desires, we saw it as our responsibility to teach them more effective ways to communicate and how to tolerate adversity. And when clients proclaimed that they enjoyed being solitary, that they didn't need friends or companions, we thought perhaps they weren't making an informed decision and therefore attempted to expose them to enjoyable social opportunities to broaden their horizons and open the door to meaningful relationships.

We taught our clients to self-advocate. They participated in their program development and attended meetings to discuss their Individual Program Plan (IPP). They helped design their programs. Not surprisingly, there were disagreements about what goals to adopt and how to prioritize them. But once again we believed it was our ethical responsibility to do what our clinical and research experiences indicated was in the best interests of our clients. Naturally, our clients had the ultimate say because they could opt out of the program. We typically found if we developed trust, formed a therapeutic alliance, carefully listened to our clients and offered rationales that were meaningful to them, then we would end up on the same page. Similarly in the medical field, patients are not mandated to follow physician's recommendations. When patients threaten to leave the hospital Against Medical Advice (AMA) the most effective physicians don't rescind the advice, but recalibrate their effort to provide meaningful rationales.

It is our strong belief that it is not appropriate or ethical to automatically honor the desires of our clients. But we will listen, seriously consider their wishes and perspective, and deeply reflect upon how to incorporate those into the final recommendations. There is a parallel in parenting. As parents, our strongest instinct is to keep our children happy, but upon consideration it is clear that we shouldn't succumb to all their wants. Their well-being should override the desire for gratification. It is critical for children to have a reasonably healthy diet, brush their teeth, go to bed at a sensible time and attend school, even if their preference is to only eat sweets, not brush their teeth, stay up as late as their parents and just play all day. Of course, with adult clients, it is the client who has the final say except in circumstances of imminent harm to themselves or another person. Otherwise, our role is to guide them to make an informed decision and they can choose whether or not to participate.

Many leaders of the rediscovery movement have modified the definition of "compassion" to include that practitioners should completely abide by the wishes of their consumers. So, if it's their preference not to have friendships, we shouldn't attempt to influence their desires. If there are topics they don't want to learn, then that's their choice. And if they want to engage in stereotypies, we should abide by their wishes. For those who are able to make an informed decision, we respect their choices and do not try to impose our views on them. But if someone comes to us asking for help, we owe it to them to share our professional guidance on more effective ways to achieve their goals and to better understand the impact of choices that they make.

For children who are unable to make an informed decision, it falls to their parents to make the judgment about what is in the child's best interest and not automatically follow the child's preference. Here is an example. Disruptive behavior works for a child. They don't see any need to change their behavior. They become solitary, have restricted interests and don't conform with social expectations because they choose to do what makes them "happy." Because they do not wish to change their behaviors, should we blindly follow their dictates? We think parents have an obligation to steer their child toward growth-producing activities and to expose their child to a broad range of life-enriching experiences. Is it compassionate to tolerate a child's violent behavior because it is a person's means of expressing frustration? If we take the position that violent behavior is inappropriate does that mean we are colluding with parents in "ableism"? We think not.

We recognize that we have a very distinct belief system that some outspoken autism advocates do not agree with. While we absolutely will listen carefully regarding consumers' desires and attempt to the best of our abilities to understand their perspectives, we believe that as interventionists (e.g., psychologists, marriage and family therapists, BCBAs), we have a duty to follow what our clinical and research experiences have shown is in the client's best interests. This may not be what clients have expressed as their desire or goals. This doesn't mean we were not reflective or compassionate listeners. It means we have a different perspective.

Some of those in the rediscovery movement have also voiced their strong opposition to coercion. We, too, disdain coercion! But we have a very different idea of what constitutes coercion. Hard-liners see coercion everywhere: from heavy-handed threats to making preferred activities contingent on externally imposed expectations, e.g., "First do your homework, then you can play video games." They see withholding reinforcement as coercive. Even praise and goodwill are viewed as coercive in nature because they represent an attempt to get someone to do something against their will. If we adhere to this definition, then we abandon the natural relationship between behavior and consequences. Everything we know about the science of behavior would become moot: reinforcers would only be provided noncontingently and thus become ineffective. To hard-liners, providing someone with corrective feedback is also considered "coercion"! In learning a skill, it is just as important to know what doesn't work as it is to know what does work. How do we help someone if we don't let them know what is thwarting their performance? How would athletes, musicians and children with autism improve without corrective feedback?

Certainly, we agree that using aversive procedures should be the last resort and only when the behavior could result in dire outcomes. But sometimes using aversive procedures is the most humane tool available. If someone is engaging in life threatening behavior, and after exhausting all possible positive procedures with no success, then it could be reasonable to consider whether there is an aversive procedure that would prevent harm. A basic example of this is crossing the street properly and safely, at the right time, in the right place. This is a complex, fundamental skill, critical to greater independence in our communities. Without this skill, those in the community would literally be risking their lives every time they stepped off a curb. This skill set can be broken down into component parts and taught, powerfully, positively, interactively and supportively. But if—after all the greatest teaching techniques were employed, and all the reinforcement and praise were utilized, even when all the support and care in the world was applied to the understanding of this concept—the learner still stepped off the curb at the wrong time, into oncoming traffic, the most moral, ethical and humane option would be to physically stop that forward momentum. And if we have to use physical force, wouldn't it also be more humane to pair it with a sufficiently loud "STOP!" that would get their attention and that we could use in the future if necessary, thereby no longer having to put hands on them? It is essential that those who have experienced trauma receive therapy. However, it must be provided by therapists who are trained and licensed clinicians. Licensed psychologists, social workers and marriage and family therapists receive extensive training in dealing with trauma, including years of education and supervised experience. Moreover, they have passed tests that qualify them to provide therapy. Being a BCBA does not qualify one to perform therapy. Attending webinars or taking classes does not qualify one to provide trauma intervention. In fact, in most states, practicing psychology without a license is illegal and unethical.

CONCLUSION

The hallmark of applied behavior *analysis* is the component of analysis, the constant, objective evaluation of techniques, theories and application through rigorous research supported under the ABA umbrella. Critical thinking is a paramount skill when embarking on any analysis: the ability to define a concept, its purpose or goals, then create a model for application, and then test it to ensure it achieves what it was meant to, efficiently, effectively, and in a replicable manner. This is the process that has led to some of the greatest innovations in ABA: teaching strategies such as discrete trial teaching, the teaching interaction procedure and task analysis; respondent interventions such as systematic desensitization, progressive relaxation techniques, individualized coping strategies and guided imagery; and reinforcement systems such as token economies, intermittent reinforcement schedules and classroom management tools. All these procedures and systems benefit those who experience them and make teaching and therapy attainable to everyone. These techniques were born of creativity and a desire to solve real world problems, but they were then extensively vetted, tested and modified. Vigilantly identifying what is effective and what we must change and even what to eliminate is core to ABA implementation and dissemination. Clearly, critical analysis is not only crucial when working with individuals, but also as a quality management procedure that should always be applied within our field. Behaviorism has been vital in helping people of all ages, cultures and walks of life. ABA has been responsible for life-saving changes and has vastly improved the quality of lives.

We need to put our past into historical perspective. We need to learn from experience and not repeat egregious errors in the future. But we should not make the sweeping generalization that all ABA is abusive and therefore should be avoided at all costs. Unfortunately, there are militant "advocates" that don't appear to be critical thinkers arriving at just such a conclusion (see Leaf et al., 2021 for an overview of this issue). Often their conclusions include outlandish embellishment and exaggeration. Examples of this hyperbole is evident all over the social network. And once those statements are typed and sent, they spread like poison coursing through veins. There is no room in an enlightened conversation for inflammatory and unjustified statements as: "All of ABA is abusive. Enrolling children in ABA programs is equivalent to sending them to the coal mines." Or, far worse, calling parents whose children are receiving ABA "murderers." There is a nefarious agenda here, and it serves no good to those who require and seek effective treatment, or for those who, with informed minds, decide to choose another path. Attempting to abolish ABA treatment for autism lacks vision and denies the right to access life-changing treatment.

As mentioned previously there are important discussions regarding "coercion" occurring in ABA. These are necessary discussions. But we must arrive at a common language and cooperatively define key concepts so we can all move forward. Pointing a gun at someone and demanding their wallet is not the same thing as "withholding" an A grade from a student who did not complete their course work successfully. The former represents extreme harm to a victim to accomplish benefit to the perpetrator. It makes sense to use the word "coercion" to describe a threat of violence, but we should not conflate it with a contingent academic letter grade or a simple social consequence such as a look of disapproval.

An understanding between interested and invested parties gives us a base to launch from, an agreement about what we are discussing and what are our common goals. This allows the conversation to be productive, respectful and forward-looking. We must monitor our field to assure that treatment is not abusive, remains progressive and effective for our clients, and meets the highest ethical standards. But we also cannot allow baseless attacks, hyperbole and misconceptions to permeate the discussion. We must not be vitriolic and caustic; this does no good. We have to promote basic decency, a willingness to listen, and move towards a treatment philosophy addressing the ills of the human condition, respectfully, in an informed manner, and cooperatively. We have to base our language on science and accountability. We need to adjust the lens to focus on where to go from here as partners.

There are several fundamental topics we can use to begin this process. Every one of us has areas of our lives we would like to change; unhealthy habits we can focus on and improve, non-social and non-inclusive thinking we can adjust and move away from. This is something we all share, no matter what our condition, religion, gender or race. To help each other with this hopeful outlook, we need to agree upon what basic behaviors we encourage as a society, and what behaviors we can identify that degrade and harm individuals and thus, worsen the greater social condition. We understand this is a fluid conversation with uncountable variables. But beginning the conversation with common language and a common goal to develop clear definitions of concepts we are discussing will allow us to then better define ways to increase or decrease those basic behaviors. Then we must carefully and thoughtfully define "coercion"—what it is and what it isn't. We cannot classify everything that results in reducing behaviors as "coercive." This would not allow for any growth, would limit self-discovery and hinder higher self-attainment. We expect that as we progress through a productive conversation, we would find agreement that coercion of the extreme variety should not occur. For example, using corporal punishment in non-life threating situations should be prohibited. Instead of painting all types of behavior influence with the same brush, we can define a continuum of restrictiveness, i.e., to what extent does a consequence result in restricting the options available to a person or inflict discomfort or inconvenience? There should be correspondence between the gravity of the behavior and the ensuing consequence. The greater the threat of harm, the greater the degree of restriction that is justified and the greater the obligation to act. There is absolutely no place in ABA for being mean, indifferent or threatening. If the literature and history of ABA were thoroughly researched, we would not find guidelines condoning cruelty, callousness, maliciousness or being unkind. The problem lies not with the philosophy, but with individual practitioners and the misuse of therapeutic tools. It lies with interpretation and delivery. There are interventionists that should simply not be in the field, just as there are police officers that are racist, doctors that are abusive, and CEOs that are narcissists. We abhor the use of ABA in a manipulative, mean or threatening manner. We must continue to police our ranks, and weed out the bad seeds, just as every profession with standards and ethics does.

We are deeply concerned about the negative experiences that too many people with autism have endured. It is one of the reasons why we have been so outspoken about poor ABA throughout our careers. But we must also recognize that those who had horrendous experiences don't speak for all adults who received treatment. Many adults have experienced high-quality treatment, are very satisfied with how it has improved their quality of life, and choose not to participate in the debate about ABA. In fact, many of them are unaware that a debate is even occurring because they don't spend time on social media sites where people are talking about autism. We implore everyone, please, "don't throw the baby out with the bathwater." When practiced correctly, ABA can be positively life-changing, so let's not abolish ABA as a treatment option. Instead, let's rid the field of ABA that is rigid and abusive. Let's improve the field. Let's make it mandatory that all interventionists be trained in clinical skills! And let's not allow militant advocates against ABA to shut down intervention for those who need it.

THE TAKEAWAY

Compassionate behaviorism and ABA are not new whatsoever. Many of our forefathers and foremothers were compassionate behaviorists. Many were empathetic and sensitive clinicians who dealt with a variety of issues affecting children, adolescents and adults. They were adept at developing therapeutic alliance, were active listeners, and skillfully dealt with resistance. They were not only well-trained in behaviorism but other schools of psychology as well. Many were licensed therapists and dealt with a myriad of issues. They were curious listeners and compassionate. That was part of their training, part of their fabric, part of their being talented clinicians. And although it is perplexing that old concepts are being seen as new, we are thrilled for the field to once again become compassionate. We can do better and as Adlai Stevenson and Barrack Obama exhorted, "We *need* to do better!"

References

Devita-Raeburn, E. (2016, August 11). *Is the most common therapy for autism cruel?* https://www.theatlantic.com/health/archive/2016/08/aba-autism-controversy/495272/

Leaf, J.B., Cihon, J.H., Leaf, R., McEachin, J., Liu, N., Russell, N., Unumb, L., Shapiro, S., Khosrowshahi, D. (2021). Concerns about ABA-based intervention: An evaluation and recommendations. *Journal of Autism and Developmental Disorders*.

Leaf, J. B., Leaf, R., McEachin, J., Taubman, M., Ala'i-Rosales, S., Ross, R. K., Smith, T, & Weiss, M. J. (2016). Applied Behavior Analysis is a Science and, Therefore, Progressive. *Journal of Autism and Developmental Disorders*, 46, 720-731.

Leaf, R. B.,McEachin, J. J., & Taubman, M. (2008). *Sense and nonsense in the behavioral treatment of autism: It has to be said.* Different Roads to Learning, NY:NY.

Leaf, R., Leaf, J. B., & McEachin, J. (2019). *Clinical judgment in ABA: Lessons from our pioneers.* Different Roads to Learning, NY:NY.

Miller, M. (2021, June). *Compassionately assessing challenging behavior.* Invited presentation for Luna ABA. Online.

Ram, J. (2020, June 2). *I am a disillusioned BCBA: Autistics are right about ABA.* https://neuroclastic.com/2020/06/02/i-am-a-disillusioned-bcba-autistics-are-right-about-aba/.

DR. RONALD LEAF is a licensed psychologist with over 45 years of experience in the field of autism. Dr. Leaf began his career working with Professor Ivar Lovaas, while receiving his undergraduate degree at University of California, Los Angeles (UCLA). Subsequently, he received his doctorate under the direction of Prof. Lovaas. During his years at UCLA, he served as Clinic Supervisor, Research Psychologist, Lecturer and Interim Director of the Young Autism Project. He was extensively involved in several research investigations, contributed to *The Me Book*, and is a co-author of *The Me Book Videotapes*. Dr. Leaf has consulted to families, schools, and agencies on a national and international basis. He is the Co-founder and Director of Autism Partnership, which offers comprehensive services for families with children and adolescents diagnosed with autism spectrum disorder (ASD). With offices in 10 countries, Ron and his team have developed the Autism Partnership Method, a progressive approach to implementing Applied Behavior Analysis (ABA) treatment. He is co-author of *A Work in Progress, Time for School, It Has to Be Said, Crafting Connections, A Work in Progress Companion Series, Clinical Judgment* and *Autism Partnership Method: Social Skills Group*. He has co-authored over 75 articles in research journals and presented over 100 times at professional conferences. Dr. Leaf is also the Co-founder of the Autism Partnership Foundation, a non-profit dedicated to advancing professional standards and treatment of individuals with autism through research and training.

JAMISON DAYHARSH is a licensed Marriage and Family Therapist. Ms. Dayharsh began working with children with autism spectrum disorder in the late 1970s at UCLA on the Young Autism Project, where she served as a Senior Therapist, Research Assistant, and Teaching Assistant. She earned her master's degree in counseling psychology at Loyola Marymount University in 1983. Ms. Dayharsh is the Executive Director of Behavior Therapy and Learning Center. Her work has included parent training and consulting nationally and internationally to parents, schools and mental health agencies. Ms. Dayharsh is an author of *A Work in Progress*, a book on behavioral treatment and a contributor to research publications. Ms. Dayharsh's expertise includes counseling families of children with disabilities as well as providing psychotherapy to children and adolescents with autism spectrum disorders.

JONATHAN RAFUSE is a Board-Certified Behavior Analyst who graduated from UCLA in 1988 with a bachelor's degree in psychology. In 1991, he received his master's degree in clinical psychology from Antioch University. He furthered his graduate studies in 2017, completing coursework at the University of North Texas. During his master's coursework he was the Clinical Director for 1736 Family Crisis Center's Youth Shelter, overseeing the intense therapy and treatment provided to runaway and abused adolescents. In 1992, he began work at the May Institute running an off-campus group home serving students dramatically impacted with ASD. In 1995, he joined Autism Partnership, which offers comprehensive services for families with children and adolescents with autism spectrum disorder (ASD), and where he is a Clinical Director. He oversees the clinical and programmatic direction of therapy teams providing treatment to this highly individualized population. His responsibilities further include advanced training, mentoring, and consultation to ABA-service providers and teaching staff within school districts and private agencies across the country. He has presented both nationally and internationally at conferences on Applied Behavior Analysis, and consults throughout the United States, Australia and Asia. He wrote chapters in *Crafting Connections* and *The Autism Partnership Method: Social Skills Groups* and contributed to the video companion series to *A Work in Progress*.

JOHN McEACHIN, a Licensed Psychologist, Licensed Behavior Analyst, and Progressive Behavior Analyst-Autism Professional, has been providing behavioral services and conducting research on autism for five decades. He received his graduate training under Professor Ivar Lovaas at UCLA on the Young Autism Project. During his 11 years at UCLA, Dr. McEachin served in various roles including Clinic Supervisor, Research and Teaching Assistant, and Instructor. His research has included the long-term follow-up study of young autistic children who received intensive behavioral treatment, which was published in 1993. In 1994 he joined with Ron Leaf in forming Autism Partnership, which they co-direct. In 1999 they published *A Work in Progress*, a widely used behavioral treatment manual and curriculum for children with ASD. Dr. McEachin has lectured throughout the world and co-authored several books and more than 100 research articles published in peer reviewed journals. Besides his clinical and research work, he is currently President of the Progressive Behavior Analyst Autism Council and an instructor in the Psychology department at Long Beach State University.

JUSTIN LEAF, Ph.D., is the Executive Director for Autism Partnership Foundation and the Progressive Behavior Analyst Autism Council, the Associate Director for ABA Doctoral Studies at Endicott College, and the Executive Director for Contemporary Behavior Consultants. Dr. Leaf received his doctorate degree in Behavioral Psychology from the Department of Applied Behavioral Science at the University of Kansas. His research interests include Progressive ABA, improving behavioral intervention, social behavior, and methodologies to improve the lives of autistic/individuals diagnosed with ASD. He has over 140 publications in either peer reviewed journals, books, or book chapters and has presented at both national and international professional conferences and invited events. He has served on numerous editorial boards for behavior analytic and autism journals. Justin's career has been dedicated to improving the field of Applied Behavior Analysis and the lives of individuals with autism.